GHOSTS OF GENESEE COUNTRY

GHOSTS OF GENESEE COUNTRY

FROM CAPTAIN KIDD TO THE UNDERGROUND RAILROAD

RALPH ESPOSITO

Haunted America

Published by Haunted America
A Division of The History Press
Charleston, SC 29403
www.historypress.net

All images by and courtesy of author unless otherwise stated.

First published 2009

Manufactured in the United States

ISBN 978.1.59629.811.8

Library of Congress Cataloging-in-Publication Data

Esposito, Ralph.
Ghosts of Genesee country : from Captain Kidd to the underground railroad / Ralph
Esposito.
p. cm.
Includes bibliographical references and index.
ISBN 978-1-59629-811-8 (alk. paper)
1. Ghosts--Genesee River Valley Region (Pa. and N.Y.) 2. Ghosts--New York (State),
Western. I. Title.
BF1472.U6E77 2009
398.209747'88--dc22
2009030572

This book is dedicated with love to my son Joseph.

CONTENTS

CONTENTS

CONTENTS

PREFACE

Where did you hear your first ghost story? Like many people, the first ghost story I heard was from my family. It is a story that I remember hearing from my childhood. My father, Raymond, and my aunt, Julie (his sister), told me this story many times, about when they were children living in Catskill, New York. My dad, aunt and a group of friends went exploring. They had found their way into an old house near Bridge Street, through an open basement window, and were exploring the dark and creepy cellar. As Ray walked past the wooden coal bin, a black hand reached out and grabbed him by the neck. Terrified, he tried to squirm out of the grasp, and as he hit the hand, he yelled, "Let me go! Let me go!"

The rest of the kids were so frightened that they all screamed and scrambled to get out of the window, leaving my dad alone struggling to get away from the hand. It lifted him off the ground and began to pull him inside the dark bin. At that moment, he heard a hiss, and a stray cat leaped from a nearby shelf onto the hand. The cat dug in with its claws, the hand released him and Ray turned and literally jumped up and out the open window.

The next day, the children's curiosities led them back to that basement. Armed with sticks, just in case the hand was still there, they went back through the window. The coal bin was empty except for a bit of coal. Next to the bin was the lifeless body of a cat, the same one that had saved my father's life.

This was my first real ghost story, even though there was a non-ghostly explanation for the hand—a unpleasant vagrant hiding in the coal bin. It did establish my interest in ghosts and the paranormal at a young age.

Growing older, I must admit to a curiosity about death and the afterlife. It is hard to imagine anyone without at least a tiny bit of interest in the afterlife. It is a question we all have wrestled with, whether you are strong in faith or an atheist.

After my dad passed away, I would go to visit my grandmother in Catskill, a small town in upstate New York, several times a year. Now, at her age, grandma's mind was forgetful at best, but she still recalled most of the family. Whenever she saw me, she would smile and tell me that my dad stops by to visit her now and then. Grandma lived to be 103. She had quite a life, outliving three of her children, including my dad.

Now Aunt Julie, who was taking care of her, just thought it was her mental state. I always wondered about that until my Aunt Fran told me this story. Still living in the family home in Brooklyn, New York, Aunt Fran now sleeps in the same room my dad had when he was a child. She told me that occasionally she wakes up and the sheets on the end of her bed are pressed down as if a child had been sitting on the bed.

She told that me she could feel my father's presence at times. I like to think he is visiting the people and places that were dear to him in life. Thinking back to my grandma, could it be that those departed relatives really did visit?

I began to get seriously interested in ghost hunting in 2003. An opportunity presented itself to join a group that was interested in the paranormal. The group began having regular meetings, and everyone shared their ghostly experiences. Well, at that time I had never really had any run-in with a ghost, but I was fascinated by their stories.

Our little group planned a few ghost hunts, starting with local cemeteries and parks. Many of the places had quite an interesting history behind them, and not just a haunted history. Several of the stories here are from those early ghost hunts.

The group picked up more members and eventually ended up at Rolling Hills Mall, the old Genesee County Poorhouse. It's quite haunted. It has been featured on one of the episodes of *Ghost Hunters* on the SyFy Channel. Part of the original group helped conduct the Rolling Hills overnight ghost hunts in the mall. As of this writing, Rolling Hills is being sold.

PREFACE

In 2004, I began doing ghost walks in the Rochester area. In putting together the stories, I became fascinated by the history of the areas, as well. Currently, we do these only in October or by appointment during the rest of the year. I enjoy doing them immensely; they are fun, and many times I learn from the guests.

In 2006, an opportunity to do a cable access show on ghost hunting came up. We called it *Mystic Encounters*, and it has aired around Monroe County. It's a lot of fun, and we have had a positive response from viewers. We have currently shot three investigations for the 2009 season.

By this time, I had been collecting ghost stories from many sources. Most are small stories that would have been forgotten in a generation. I found many of the stories interesting, some funny and some very touching. I felt that they should be shared with those who are interested. I hope you enjoy them.

I would like to thank the many people who helped me with this project. First, all the kind people who have shared their wonderful stories with me. It's not always easy to tell anyone about your encounter with a ghost.

A special thank-you to all the friends who encouraged and helped me to write this book, especially Frank, Shelly, Gail, Kathy and the gang with whom I go ghost hunting. They each shared their unique talents, helped me gather the stories and helped write, polish and publish them.

If you have a ghost story that has happened to you or your family and would like to share it with me, please write me at reparanormal@rochester.rr.com.

INTRODUCTION

This book is a collection of true ghost stories. It is also a book with a bit of the history of the Genesee country. All of the ghost stories in this book are either from my own experiences or were told to me by people on one of my investigations or ghost walks. They experienced the "ghost" firsthand. In most stories, I changed the names of the living and give only the street name to respect the privacy of the families.

To check the accuracy of many of the stories, I went to the actual location with a psychic, who was told nothing of the stories. They were asked their impressions of each location. The amazing thing is how close the psychic's impressions often were to the stories. In some cases, the ghosts would actually "tell" their story, and I have included several of the ghosts' stories. In addition, I went to local historians in order to verify the names and other details of the stories.

One thing I have found is that there are a lot of ghost stories out there —not just famous legends like "The White Lady of Durand Eastman Park"; those are the ones everyone hears about. These are the small ones, ones that still deserve to be told and remembered.

Are ghosts real? That is for you to decide for yourself. I just hope you enjoy the stories. As for me, my money is on the ghosts.

PART I

GENESEE
COUNTRY NORTH

ROCHESTER

Much of western New York is considered Genesee country. For the scope of this book, I narrowed it down a bit to the areas closer to the Genesee River. Geologically, Genesee country was created by the last ice age. Like giant hands, the glacial sheets sculpted the land as they advanced and receded, creating the Genesee Valley. Through it runs the mighty Genesee River, flowing north from its headwaters in what is now Pennsylvania. It's one of the few rivers in the world that flow north; also on this shortlist is the Nile.

The story of Genesee country is steeped in a rich and somewhat bloody history. The Seneca Indians called it the "good" or "pleasant valley." The first white men came to the area back in the mid-1600s when the French first set foot ashore in what is now called Irondequoit, a Mohawk Indian term meaning "where land and waters meet." Because of its location and rich resources, this area was fought over by the Native Americans, French, English and Americans—wars for greed, conquest, territory and independence.

The really big settlement period began in the1790s, when the westward expansion was initiated to inhabit the Genesee region of New York State. Called "Genesee Fever" (not to be confused with the "fevers" that many sickened and died from in the area because of mosquito-spread illness), this migration rush came from New England. They were pioneers hungry for virgin land. This was the frontier back then, waiting to be tamed, settled, the land cleared and crops planted, not to mention the vast resources of timber to be logged. These were hearty men and women who, despite hardships, weather, wild animals, disease and Native Americans who were not always happy to see them, managed to hew a place in this wilderness for themselves and their families.

The Genesee River as it flows today through downtown Rochester.

The central area for this book is Rochester, New York. First called Rochesterville, it was formed in 1816 and grew to eventually swallow up a number of nearby settlements and several ports including Kings Landing, Carthage and Tryon City. As it grew, it dropped the "ville," and Rochester became a growing metropolitan area.

As with any book on ghosts, I would be remiss not to mention Rochester, New York, as the nexus of the spiritualist movement. The three Fox sisters who lived in Hydesville, a small town east of Rochester, claimed to have communicated with the ghost of a dead peddler through a code using knocks. They claimed he had been murdered and buried in the basement of their home years prior to their family buying the house. Their father dug up the portion of the basement where his daughters said the peddler had been buried. He did unearth an old peddler's case and some human bones. News of the sister's ability to communicate with the deceased spread quickly. In the early 1800s, the Fox sisters became celebrated mediums in Rochester and throughout both the United States and Europe. They would conduct public séances, at which they would contact the spirits. This was the beginning of the spiritualist movement. By 1885, there were many charlatans doing spirit medium scams with a corresponding increase in investigations of fraud. Even the Fox sisters were under suspicion of being fakes. This caused the public's interest in mediums to wane. There was a dedicated following, though, and that continues even today. As a religion, the spiritualist church is still active.

Some followers of the Fox sisters' spiritualist movement went on to settle in Lily Dale, New York, south of Buffalo. To this day Lily Dale is a community of spiritualists and holds many seminars and meetings dealing with spiritualism and related topics.

The Fox home is located in Hydesville, New York, and only the foundation is left, which is being preserved. You may visit the site and see the foundation. There is a glass-enclosed pavilion around it so visitors can look in. Their home in Rochester did not fare so well; it was torn down to make room for an expressway ramp. Let nothing stand in the way of progress.

Genesee country was once known as the "Burned-Over District." This meaning did not reflect fires that burned down buildings but rather the fires in people's souls. The religious fervor was extensive—some might even go so far as to call some of them cults. They began and swept through the region in the 1800s. This included the start of "religious" groups such as the Latter-Day Saints movement, Millerites, Oneida Society, spiritualists, Shakers, Mormons, Free Methodists and others.

Not only does Genesee country have an interesting history, it also has a large population of ghosts and, of course, ghost stories.

"Indian" Allan and the Flour City

When the first settlers came to the area, it was very swampy and a source of mosquitoes. The little winged bloodsuckers spread "swamp fevers" such as malaria. These fevers would sicken and kill many of the new settlers in the area. Kings Landing on the Genesee River was abandoned when most of the residents died of the "fever." Eventually, the swamps were drained or filled in, and the mosquitoes were brought under control, as well as the threat of the fever.

There were many swampy areas in Genesee Country full of wildlife and disease-bearing insects.

One of the early pioneers in the area when it was still wilderness was Ebenezer "Indian" Allan, a colorful rogue if ever there was. Tales of his wild behavior include adultery, polygamy, swindling and murder. He was a friend and blood brother of the Iroquois Indians, and having taken an Indian woman as his first companion/wife, Ebenezer became known as "Indian" Allan.

Originally a Tory (British) sympathizer in the Revolutionary War, he joined Butler's Rangers (also British), who raided white settlements from the Susquehanna to the Genesee Valley. Allan gained a reputation as a savage fighter, viciously killing men, women and children indiscriminately on the raids. Allan fought with the British until he realized that the British would not win.

A pragmatic man, he decided to switch sides. Allan stole a sacred wampum belt and gave it to the American Indian commissioner. The belt enabled the commissioner safe passage to forge a peace treaty with the Iroquois and the new American government. Allan's motive was to spare his Indian brothers more bloodshed.

The British sent a group of soldiers and Indians to hunt him down for the theft of the wampum. Allan was captured and brought to Fort Niagara, near Lewiston, New York. A fire mysteriously started in the stockade in which he was locked, and Ebenezer took the distraction to make his escape.

Allan made his way to the Philadelphia peace council that was being held to propose an armistice with the Indian nations. Allan knew that it would mean a bloody war if an agreement was not reached. While he was in Philadelphia, a mob of furious Fort Wilkes-Barre settlers remembered "Indian" Allan from the brutal raids on their homes by Butlers Rangers. Wasting no time, they grabbed some rope and chased him with the intent to stretch his neck. Ebenezer, being rather fond of the current length of his neck, made a narrow escape and returned to his home, Allan's Hill, now called Mount Morris, in New York. Shortly after his return, the British recaptured him and held him in Montreal, Quebec, until 1784. After his release, he came back to his home in Genesee country.

Among his other escapades included the time a newly married couple was looking to settle in the Allan's Hill area. They came to his cabin, and Allan welcomed them. It seems that Ebenezer found the young wife, Christine, quite attractive. He told the couple of a wondrous gorge, known today as the Genesee Gorge, with a beautiful waterfall. Allan invited the husband to go and see the river and falls with him.

The two men set off in the morning, and by late afternoon, Allan returned carrying the husband, who was very wet and grievously injured. With a sad look on his face, Allan told Christine that her husband had been looking at the splendor of the river when the most horrible thing happened: the edge gave way. Her husband fell in and was almost lost in the swirling waters of the river. Most accounts suggest that Ebenezer actually hit the poor gentleman over the head and pushed him in, but Allan recounted the mishap somewhat differently. The tale told was how he, without thought to his own well-being, jumped in and pulled her husband to safety. He comforted the wife and assured her that they could stay there until he recovered. The husband died several days later. Ebenezer continued to comfort the new widow and extended his home to her until arrangements to go back east could be made.

Christine had little choice but to accept Allan's kind offer and stayed a year with him and his Indian wife, Sally. Apparently, Ebenezer had a liking for having more than one woman living with him, for besides his Indian wife he also married several white women, Mille McGregor and Lucy Chapman. One can only imagine that the lonely and rugged pioneer life seemed to make such communal living arrangements easier to accept.

Allan was contracted to build the first gristmill where Rochester is now located. Indeed, it was his mill that Colonel Nathaniel Rochester saw when he traveled to the area in 1811. It convinced the colonel of the feasibility of using the river and falls for industry and influenced him to establish Rochesterville on that site.

Allan eventually sold his land holdings here and moved to upper Canada, where he went bankrupt. Ebenezer "Indian" Allan died in 1816; the original millstones from his gristmill are today part of the second-floor wall of the former county courthouse on West Main Street, where visitors can see and even touch the stones that ground the first grain in Rochester.

After the Revolutionary War, Virginian Colonel Nathaniel Rochester purchased one hundred acres of land (1803) on the Genesee River; eight years later, he established the small settlement of Rochesterville. He knew that it had promise as a prime location because of the three great pillars of real estate—location, location and location. Well, in this case, it was the three waterfalls on the river offering great potential for industry using water power. Power was an important natural commodity for a new community in the wilderness.

In 1817, Colonel Rochester served on a committee to petition the state to build the Erie Canal on the proposed northern route that went through Rochesterville. Because Rochesterville had the river and its falls to support industry, it was a good bet. In 1823, the Erie Canal came through, ensuring prosperity and growth for the settlement. Thus, Rochesterville became

An old foundation and water raceway that were used for power on the Genesee River.

Rochester. By 1828, Rochester had ten flour mills, eight hotels and nine sawmills and was home port for 160 canalboats.

Nathaniel Rochester became the first county clerk and later the first New York State assemblyman from the area. As the man who literally founded Rochester, he also helped establish many local churches, banks and academic institutions—important to the success of the area well into the future.

Originally called the Flour City because of the water-powered flour mills, the area started to export flour from local mills in 1815 and continued until the Great Plains became the major wheat growing area of our nation. Rochester became the Flower City in the twentieth century because of its beautiful parks and plant nurseries.

The Lost City of Tryon

The Lost City of Tryon. Sounds like a movie title. In it, an old adventurer like Errol Flynn swings his machete at the thick green leaves. The heavy leaves fall away to reveal the legendary lost city of Tryon!

The real city of Tryon was never lost, nor was it ever really a city. It was one man's gamble that was lost: John Tryon purchased the land around what was then called Indian Landing, now Ellison Park, in Monroe County, New York, in 1797. At the time he started, Tryon City was an oasis of civilization in the wilderness, but progress can change everything.

It is appropriate that I start with a historic marker that relates some of the area's history:

> *The most important place in the early history of the Genesee Country, all of whose trails led to Irondequoit Bay. A gateway of the Iroquois Confederacy. Here were scenes of adventure and romance for more than 300 years, involving Indian wars, the struggle for empire between the French and English and the Revolutionary and pioneer period. Religion, commerce and war made this territory a famous battleground, bringing here many noted traders, priests and soldiers.*

From the Marquis de Denonville marching through the area in 1687 in a war to wipe out the Seneca Indians over the fur trade routes to the settlers

Ganondagan, a large Seneca town near present-day Victor, New York. The Marquis de Denonville destroyed it in 1687 to secure the fur trade route through the area. Ganondagan had over one hundred long houses and grain storage buildings that were burned to the ground as the French marched through the area to destroy the Seneca and control the land.

coming in the 1800s, the ground of western New York is steeped in blood, ambition and history. Such famous units as Rogers' Rangers tread the same paths that are today used by hikers, joggers and others.

In 1721, the British sent Captain Peter Schuyler and nine others, who were Dutch, to spy on the French in this area. They came here under the auspices of setting up a trading post at Indian Landing. Unlike today, the creek at that time was both wider and deeper; Indian Landing was the spot at which thirty-ton cargo schooners could dock. It got its name because it was a convenient place to trade with the local Indians. They built a log structure that became known as Fort Schuyler near what is today the Frisbee Golf Course. Captain Schuyler and the others abandoned the fort after only a year.

It was a new nation and a new era of big ideas—and a vast wilderness in which to build them. In 1797, a man named John Tryon purchased the two hundred acres around Indian Landing on Irondequoit Creek. It was an important place not only because it was a port but also because the creek's water power could be harnessed for industry.

In Tryon's time, goods and people came either overland by poor roads or trails, or by boat. A port could get regular and relatively fast deliveries of goods and also ship out what the area produced in all but the worst weather and winter ice over. Tryon's dream was to build a town on Indian Landing and call it Tryon City.

Soon, Tryon City had a dry goods store, a blacksmith's shop, a shoe factory, a distillery, a tavern, a tannery, an ashery (which processed hardwood ashes into potash and pearlash, both important forms of alkali, which was needed for the manufacturing of textiles, glass, tanned leather, gunpowder, paper, soap and other goods), a large gristmill, a shipyard, a school, five-story warehouses and a cemetery. In those early days, Tryon City was the only settlement between Oswego and Lewiston that was near Lake Ontario.

John Tryon died in 1808, and that was a serious blow to the growth of Tryon City. It had never attracted as large a number of residents as Tryon had hoped, and with the building of the Erie Canal that bypassed Tryon for Rochesterville, much of the trade began to fall off. By 1823, Rochesterville was drawing more and more business and became the city of Rochester, and Tryon City was abandoned to the weeds.

Eventually, the land on which Tryon City had been built was swallowed up by the growing city of Rochester and became what is now Ellison Park. All that is left of the settlement are a couple of markers, several of the original homes built by the settlers and an old log cabin replica trading post where Fort Schuyler once stood.

While our memory of Indian Landing and Tryon City is almost gone (it is all but a few lines in the history books), it seems that some of the original residents are more determined not to be forgotten.

By day, it is a lovely area: a lazy creek winding through parkland. By night, a stranger feeling is prevalent. The ghosts of the area—Native Americans, pioneers and military—all died trying to tame and keep the area. I will tell you of two specters I met there one evening.

My friend Shelly, a very gifted psychic, enjoys ghost hunting. I was curious to see what she would pick up in the park. I had been there several

The Erie Canal bypassed Tryon City, a misfortune from which the settlement would not recover.

times before with another ghost hunting group, and there seemed to be lots of activity.

We parked, and before we got out of the car Shelly was aware of a ghost nearby. He walked up to her dressed in a blue military uniform with an insignia. While I could not see him, the hair on my arms was standing on end. She said that he was looking at us, wondering about our strange conveyance.

Shelly said that he seemed a little confused and agitated as he told us that our lives were in mortal danger as the Indians are waiting to ambush anyone who went down the path.

He began to tell her what had happened to his patrol. He was leading a patrol to the nearby hill so they could watch the area. As they quietly walked the trail, the Indians attacked from the heavy undergrowth. He winced in pain as an arrow tore into his shoulder, and he slowly fell forward, watching in horror as many of his men also fell. After the first flight of arrows, the warriors attacked hand-to-hand with tomahawks and war clubs. The brave patrol fought just as savagely against its attackers, who had the advantage in numbers. They killed several warriors, wounding others, as they fell one by one to the last man.

When the short but bloody ambush was over, the warriors checked the soldiers to make sure that they were all dead. They quickly dispatched any survivors with a crushing blow from a war club. The sergeant, weak from his wound, closed his eyes and feigned death, silently praying that they would miss him. As the Indians left, he staggered up and headed back to report.

The sergeant thought that his feint had worked and didn't realize the Indians had not been fooled; his lifeless body lay with his men on that path so many years ago. His last thoughts were that he must get back to report what happened and give warning. He also wanted to be sure that his men's bodies were recovered and given a proper burial.

Now he wanders the path, telling anyone who will listen to go back, that hostile Indians are nearby waiting to ambush anyone on the trail. As for his being a bit confused, well, getting hit with a war club might confuse the best of us.

I stood there listening to Shelly talk with the ghost when I felt a sensation like a soft hand touching my hair.

"Shelly," I whispered.

When Shelly looked over, she chuckled and said, "I see one found you too."

It was an oddly soothing feeling. She told me that she saw the spirit of a young Indian girl stroking my hair and softly speaking to me. Her words I could not hear, but her gentle fingers were another matter entirely. She was attracted by my hair; Shelly said it was like her husband's. The young girl was searching for him and hoped I might know where her husband was.

Early one morning, her husband had set out from the village for the place the white men called Indian Landing. He was hoping to trade some of his handcrafted jewelry with the white traders at the landing. He hoped to get a new knife and several other items for the jewelry.

Another brave was to go with him that morning, but his friend was not able. There was always a danger of going alone through the woods, as occasionally small groups of Huron would come into the Seneca's land to raid and plunder. The Huron were the enemy of the Seneca.

He had no problems getting to Indian Landing. The jewelry fetched a nice trade: the new knife he had wanted, an iron pot for his wife and several

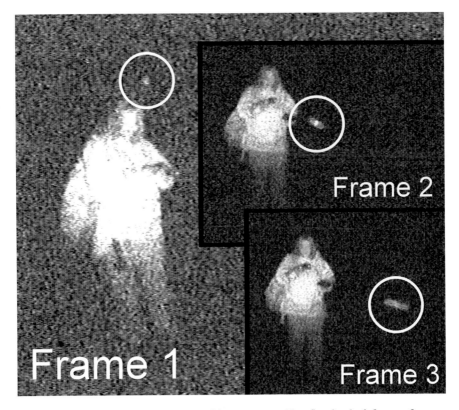

During an investigation of the old Tryon City area, something flew by the left arm of a member of one of our groups. Here are three frames that show it; the "wings" with lines are not really wings but rather artifacts from the analog infrared recording. No one heard, saw or felt anything when it "flew" by.

other metal goods. It was time to return home. He was alone on the trail about one hour from the landing when four Huron braves jumped out of the underbrush, surrounding him. They fell upon him, and though he struggled valiantly, they quickly overpowered and killed him. They dragged his body off the trail. The Hurons divided up the trade goods he had received and then hid his body so it would be difficult to find. It would give them more time without alerting the Seneca that they were there.

When her husband did not return, the tribe sent out a group of braves to search for him. They came back with no news, only that he had made it to Indian Landing and traded with the white traders there. Though suspicious, they had found no sign of the ambush.

His wife cried and mourned the loss of her husband. Today, she still searches for him at the Indian Landing where he was last seen. If you feel a soft hand touching your hair while playing Frisbee golf at Ellison Park, perhaps it is his widow still looking for her husband, remembering the hair of her beloved husband that she longs to touch again.

We left shortly after that, wondering how many other stories lie in the lost city of Tryon.

The Ugly Old Lady

Kim and her family had just moved into a single-family house on Grand Avenue near Culver Road in the city of Rochester. It was an average older home, like most of the houses on the street. The area used to be farmland but had long since been turned into a residential neighborhood.

One evening, Kim was lying on the couch watching TV, and her mother was standing at the foot of the couch talking to her. Suddenly, her mother's eyes widened, and she stopped talking in the middle of her sentence. A moment later, she blurted out, "Don't turn around!"

Kim looked at her and slowly turned her head around. Standing just behind the couch was an old woman; her skin was wrinkled, and she wore a shabby old dress. Kim was more shocked than frightened to see the woman standing there; the real thought running through her mind was "what an ugly old lady."

The old woman looked down at her and then turned around, slowly walked across the living room and disappeared when she entered the kitchen. Both Kim and her mother looked at each other and almost simultaneously yelled "Oh my God!"

That was the start of fairly frequent appearances of the old woman. When she appeared, she would usually wander the house, stopping at the photographs on the wall and looking at them. Then she would walk up to anyone who was there and watch them for a short while before walking away to the kitchen and disappearing. It was almost as if she was trying to figure out who the people were and why they were in her house.

Kim could feel the old woman's presence most strongly in the basement when she wasn't wandering the house. It was an old fieldstone basement, dark and cool. The family didn't go down there unless they absolutely had to.

One day, Kim's cousin, Robert, came over. He had heard his cousin talk about the ugly old lady and wanted to see her for himself. They told him she lived in the basement, and he would have to go down there to see her. He smiled and headed confidently to the basement door.

He descended the creaky wooden steps into the basement. With each step he felt less confident and more uneasy. As soon as he stepped onto the basement floor, he felt cold. He started to walk to the center of the floor when the hair on the back of his neck stood up. He had a feeling that someone was right behind him. Turning around, he saw the ugly old lady. She stood there in her shabby dress, just looking at him. For a moment, he was frozen as she looked into his eyes, and then he bolted for the stairs.

Accounts vary on whether he screamed as he ran up the stairs—he, of course, denies it. His grandmother stopped him as he rushed through the door from the basement. His face was ashen, he looked scared out of his wits and he was gasping for breath. Everyone in the room started to laugh, and even grandma, who was trying to comfort him, had a smile on her face. Kim said, "I see you met the ugly old lady."

Guess Who's Coming to Dinner

Back in the early '70s, on Campbell Street in Rochester, there was an old house built in the 1800s. It was a time when the area was farmland, and the house quietly stood there while time changed everything around it. Gone were the fields of crops, replaced by asphalt roads and rows of houses.

Marc was invited over for dinner by his two friends, Kevin and Linda. As Kevin fussed over his homemade sauce on the stove, the three friends enjoyed some wine and conversation in the large eat-in kitchen. As they chatted, the basement door loudly opened and closed. The couple glanced at each other, and Marc asked if they were expecting more company for dinner. Linda just smiled in a very peculiar manner, and Kevin made a nervous chuckle and continued what he was saying.

Marc began to have an unsettled feeling in his stomach—just a bit hungry, he thought, and he poured another glass of the red wine. Dinner was soon ready: salad and pasta with Kevin's homemade sauce. As Linda began serving dinner, the lights began to flicker. She looked up and said, "Stop that!" Immediately the lights came back on.

Marc looked at her and then reached for the grated cheese. As his hand reached for the jar, it moved quickly away from his grasp. "What the…all right, what's going on guys?" Marc exclaimed.

"Some more wine?" Kevin offered. Just as he said that, a glass from the dish strainer fell to the floor and smashed. As Marc looked at the fallen glass, the silverware drawer opened and fell on the floor. He looked over to Linda with a strange, quizzical look.

As they ate, Linda began to tell Marc about the house and the strange things that had happened since they had moved in. The doors opening and closing, lights flickering, objects moving and, at times, the stove burners turning on. Kevin had done some research and found that the original owner had passed away in the house, as did the child of a past owner.

Marc kept in touch with the couple and, a few years later, learned that the house had burnt down; luckily no one was home at the time. The fire department traced the fire to the stove, where the burners had been left on high. Both Kevin and Linda swore that they had checked the stove before they left, and all the burners had been off. Perhaps the ghost felt out of place in a world so changed from the simple farm of so many years ago.

The Old Milk Wagon

In the 1960s, Andrea lived with her family near Silver Stadium, the old ball park built in 1929. Originally named Red Wing Stadium, it was home of the Rochester Red Wings, as well as the New York Black Yankees of the Negro National League for their final season in 1948. It was renamed Silver Stadium in 1968 to honor Morrie Silver, who was instrumental in keeping the Red Wings in Rochester in 1957. By the 1990s, Silver Stadium was showing its age and was not up to the standards of newer stadiums. A new baseball stadium, Frontier Field, was built and opened in 1995. Sadly, historic Silver Stadium was torn down in 1997.

Andrea had an older brother, Tom. He worked for Kodak and rose before dawn for work each morning. As he got ready for work, the sound would wake Andrea, and she would lie in bed until he left the house. She would then go to her window and listen.

She would hear her brother shut the front door, walk a few steps and then pause. Out of the predawn darkness came the sound of iron horseshoes on the cobblestone street. It was a sound that had not been heard for thirty or forty years in that area. Cars and trucks, as well as asphalt, had long since replaced horse-drawn wagons and carriages on cobblestone streets.

Tom would wait quietly as the apparition of an old milk wagon pulled along by horse passed by the house. The mare's iron shoes made a slow *clop clop* sound as it passed the house. For a moment it was surreal, listening to the horse and occasionally catching a glimpse of the milk wagon as it went by. It was like going back in time. As the sounds of the horse and wagon faded, the spell was broken and he would start off for work.

To Andrea, the slow *clop clop* of the ghostly milkman's horse was a part of the morning. With that sound, she would smile, knowing that her brother was off to work.

A Day at the Races

Park Avenue was originally part of a harness racing track called the Union Park Racetrack, which was opened before the Civil War. Horses from all over the state were run at the racetrack. Next to the track on East Avenue stood the Union Tavern, where the gentlemen could enjoy a wee drop after the races. The track was broken up and sold as parcels in 1870. Vick Park A and Vick Park B are where the north and south portions of the old racetrack used to be.

Today, the area is very trendy, with lovely older homes and businesses. On Vick Park A is the Plymouth Spiritualist Church. They trace their roots to the Fox sisters and the beginning of the spiritualist movement in Rochester. They have meetings several days a week, but once in a while at the Thursday evening meetings, strange things can happen.

The meeting was going well when the sound of an old-fashioned band was heard. The music seemed to be coming from outside. The congregation looked around, and suddenly a horse snorted, and the sound of crowds of people was everywhere. Several of the more sensitive psychics in the meeting could actually see the crowd. It was like opening a door into the past: men in formal attire with top hats and ladies in fancy dress all walking around the old Union Park Racetrack.

Soon the sound of the horses' hooves pounding the track as they raced by could be heard above the excited crowd. It was a day at the races as the band played on.

The Canary House

Painted a bright canary yellow, the Canary House sits on Reservoir Avenue, near Mount Hope Avenue and Mount Hope Cemetery. The curious thing is that the front door appears to be on the east side of the house, not the north side that faces the street. This is because when it was built, there was another street on the east side, Virginia Terrace, that ran from Highland Avenue to Reservoir Avenue.

It is a lovely old house, as many of the houses on the block are, dating back to the 1800s. A lovely façade hid what was going on inside— or, more accurately, in the basement. Rumors abound in that area of tunnels that ran from house to house and even to the cemetery and the Genesee River beyond. The Canary House was said to have had a lot of activity in the basement, as it supposedly had tunnels running north to the Warner Castle and west to the cemetery and the river. They would be perfect to hide and move illegal rum and other contraband to and from the river.

Were the tunnels also used as a stop on the Underground Railroad? It is documented that there were homes in that area used to hide runaway slaves. Indeed, Frederick Douglass himself lived not far from the Canary House. Douglass, a slave who escaped to freedom, was one of the most famous abolitionists. When he lived in Rochester, he published the *North Star*, an antislavery publication. He also was a public speaker, author and statesman. In 1872, his home on South Avenue burned down. Arson was suspected, possibly set by those who did not share his abolitionist views. Frederick Douglass died in 1895 and is buried in Mount Hope Cemetery within sight of the Canary House.

Years ago, a friend of mine named Judy lived for a while in the Canary House. It was a boardinghouse at the time, and she did house cleaning for a

The Canary House on Reservoir Avenue, Rochester, New York.

bit off her rent. Soon after she moved in, Judy began noticing strange things happening in the house.

As she cleaned one of the second-floor bedrooms, she heard the sound of a horse walking down the street and then a horse snorting; it seemed to be coming from the opened window. She went to the window and looked out, but there were no horses to be seen. Puzzled, she closed the window and continued her work. She left to get some new sheets for the bed from the linen closet down the hall. When she returned, she started fitting the clean sheets when a cool breeze hit her arm. The window that she had closed a few minutes before was open again. There was no one upstairs but Judy at that time.

As time went on, more interesting occurrences began to happen. Every once in a while, a door would slam shut or a light would turn on or off. Judy asked the owners, and they would smile and joke, "Oh, that's just the ghost." The thought of working in a haunted house did not bother her; to the contrary, Judy found it fascinating.

A few days after that, Judy was in the hall off the kitchen when she was startled to see a black woman walking down the hall. She was dressed in an old-fashioned cotton dress with a white apron and scarf on her head. The apparition walked right by Judy, glancing at her briefly, and then disappeared as she entered the kitchen.

The owners also told her of the tunnels that used to be connected to the basement. They had long since been closed off and forgotten. When Judy went into the basement, she immediately felt coldness envelop her; it was the only place in the house in which she felt uncomfortable. She described it as an almost palpable fear. She always wondered if it was because slaves were hidden down there as part of the Underground Railroad.

In other rooms, she noticed furniture moved in between her going in and out of the room. Judy got the feeling that one of the ghosts liked to play pranks. Occasionally, small objects she laid down would be moved— not far but just enough that she had to look around the room to find them.

In the living room, a lovely old a mirror hung over the fireplace mantel. That Christmas, Judy was helping decorate the living room. She was trimming the mirror in garland and gazed into it. The scene that reflected back was not the living room she was decorating. Like looking through a window into the past, it was the same living room but with a lovely fresh pine tree decorated in ribbon and old-fashioned ornaments. Judy stared mesmerized by the scene; it was like a nostalgic Norman Rockwell painting. It lasted but a few moments, and then the vision faded into the reflection of the present living room.

Judy has moved many times since then; she has continued to run into ghosts, but none quite like the ones she met in the Canary House.

Some Like it Hot

On the corner of Gregory Street and South Avenue is an older brick building. Over the years, there were a number of different stores that had rented the building, including a movie theatre. In the '70s, there was a fire, and one eyewitness remembers seeing the smoke and flames from her room at Highland Hospital almost one mile down South Avenue. It damaged the building, and several people perished in the conflagration. The building

Rehabilitated today, several residents died in this building during a fire back in the 1970s.

was repaired, and today has several businesses on the main floor, as well as apartments on the upper floors.

Pat was visiting her friend, who worked in one of the stores. She asked Pat if she could throw some towels in the laundry downstairs in the basement. Pat grabbed the basket and went downstairs. It had that typically cool, slightly damp feeling that older basements often have. She walked through the door that divided the basement to get to the laundry area. In the section with the washer, she walked into an area that felt like a hot oven—so hot it felt like her skin was burning.

She hurried to the washing machine and put the load in and then ran back through the area of heat and out the door. She turned to look, and in the very spot she had just run through was a woman sitting in a chair, watching her. Pat was shocked; no one had been there when she ran through a moment ago. Then she noticed that the space around the woman looked like the air itself was on fire. Pat rushed upstairs.

Her friend took one look at her and asked, "Did you see something down there?" Pat told her what had just happened. Her friend nodded, told her the story of the fire and said that several others have had similar experiences in the basement.

Watch Over Me

Talk to most nurses who work in any hospital, and they will tell you of times when strange things happened at work. One nurse saw white shapes that visited the rooms of patients on the geriatric floor she worked. She told me that when she saw them gather at one room, that patient would usually pass away during the night. She kept her sightings to herself because the other nurses would say, "I don't want to hear it!"

This story took place at Strong Memorial Hospital, one of Rochester's finest hospitals. Interestingly enough, it sits across from Mount Hope Cemetery—perhaps not the most cheerful view for patients on that side of the hospital. Pete was an EMT. He was on night duty when he got the call that his son, Jake, was taken to Strong Memorial Hospital with a severe asthma attack. Pete hurriedly notified his ambulance headquarters as he headed straight for the hospital.

He rushed into emergency, where his son was being treated. After checking on his status, Pete apologized that he could not get there sooner. Jake smiled and said, "It's OK Dad; Grandma was here keeping me company. She told me everything would be alright."

Pete looked at him strangely and asked where she was. Jake said, "Grandma told me she had to go now but that you would be here in a minute."

Pete said, "That was nice of your mom's parents to come over right away." His son said, "No dad, it was your mom." Pete looked at his son curiously and said, "OK."

A few hours later, Jake was released from the hospital, and Pete took his son home. When they got there, Jake went right to a picture of his grandmother and her second husband that was on the wall. He pointed to it and said, "They both were there at the hospital, Grandma did the talking. They looked just as they do here in this picture."

A strange feeling came over Pete as he looked at the picture of his mom and her second husband. They had both died years ago, before Jake was even born.

ROCHESTER CEMETERIES

Rochester and the surrounding area have many great cemeteries, big and small; some date from the 1700s. I have stories from two of our most famous cemeteries. The first takes place in Holy Sepulcher Cemetery. Holy Sepulcher was the undertaking of Catholic Bishop McQuaid, who purchased the property in 1871. It was opened several years later for burials.

One of the more colorful local residents buried in Holy Sepulcher was Rattlesnake Pete. He owned Rattlesnake Pete's Saloon & Museum located in downtown Rochester in the late 1800s. Pete would go on snake hunts to collect rattlesnakes and blacksnakes. He not only decorated his saloon with

Headstones in Mount Hope Cemetery.

The chapel at the north gate of Mount Hope Cemetery. Some say that they can see a face looking out the right window over the door in the central tower.

their skins but also used them to "cure" people's ailments by wrapping one of his black snakes (nonpoisonous) around the ailing person's neck. There is more on Rattlesnake Pete in the "Gates" section.

Holy Sepulcher may also be the final resting place of one of the most infamous murderers in history. The man is Dr. Francis Tumblety, a self-proclaimed doctor specializing in female patients. The good doctor moved around the country and Europe practicing medicine. The reason he moved so frequently was that he was usually one step ahead of the law due to complaints about his medical practice. Tumblety also had a rather unusual collection of women's internal organs preserved in glass jars. The organs' original owners were unknown. His time spent in London coincides with

An enlargement from the chapel picture; is it a face or just the play of light and shadow?

the murder spree of that infamous serial killer known as Jack the Ripper in Whitechapel, England. To this day, speculation swirls around him that he was Jack the Ripper.

Mount Hope is one of our oldest cemeteries. It has one of the most unique settings of any cemetery I have ever seen: almost two hundred acres of hills, small glens, winding eskers and kettles—a landscaping courtesy of the last ice age. The cemetery was incorporated in 1838 as the first municipal cemetery in the country. The monuments include Egyptian obelisks, miniature Greek temples, mausoleums built into the hillsides, winged angels and broken columns; in addition, several buildings with Gothic towers give it an air of haunted ground.

As mentioned in the story of the Canary House, rumors persist that there are tunnels linking some of the nearby houses to locations in the cemetery and beyond where rum and other goods were smuggled. The University of

Rochester and Genesee River lie just beyond the cemetery. The area was also a possible route for the Underground Railroad. Frederick Douglass lived just down the street.

Mount Hope is also the resting place for many famous people including founder of Rochester Nathaniel Rochester, pioneer for women's suffrage Susan B. Anthony, famous abolitionist Frederick Douglass, John Jacob Bausch and Henry Lomb (of Bausch & Lomb), Hiram Sibley (involved in Western Union and the purchase of Alaska) and many, many more.

Waving Goodbye

A young woman told me this story about her grandfather. Granddad had a wonderful garden; he loved growing flowers and vegetables. The family would visit every Sunday, and he and Grandma would be out working in the garden. They would pull in behind their green Chevrolet sedan and honk the horn, and their grandparents would look up, smile and wave hello. Even from a distance, there was no mistaking Granddad; he had his own distinctive manner of waving.

Granddad passed away, and Grandma would go to visit his grave at Holy Sepulcher Cemetery every Sunday. She would carefully tend the flowers she planted by his headstone. One day she had brought several of his favorite flowers to plant at the base of his headstone. She began talking to her husband, and her eyes teared up as she told him how much she loved and missed him. She carefully dug the soil to plant the flowers.

The cemetery was silent and she was alone. Just as Grandma told him how much she missed seeing him wave, the sound of a car caught her attention. Out of nowhere, a green car drove past. She looked up. The car seemed blurred, but the driver was familiar: an older man who smiled and waved as he drove past—yes, it was that unique wave of Granddad's! Then, in the blink of an eye, the car and driver disappeared.

Grandma sat back and stared at the air where the car had vanished. She smiled and had a warm feeling inside, one that hadn't been there since her husband had passed away.

Are You Warm Yet?

I do ghost walks in and around Rochester. On one of them, we go along the fence of Mount Hope Cemetery. Mount Hope is a majestic Victorian cemetery full of beautiful memorials, obelisks, sarcophagi, mausoleums, crypts, headstones and more—all set in a most bizarre landscape of hills, sinkholes and winding roads.

One cold October night on a ghost walk, Donna, one of the guests, told me that she was getting warm on her left side. As we walked on, she reported getting warmer and warmer. We were unable to figure out why she was so warm. By the end of our walk, Donna was getting very hot on her left side.

We chatted for a while after the ghost walk ended. She told me that she was empathic, a person who can often literally feel another's emotion or pain. This is not limited to the living souls around her, for she can also feel the pain and anguish felt by the departed.

As an example of her empathic ability, Donna then told me of a trip she and her friend had taken to Gettysburg. She was walking on Baltimore Street by the house in which Jennie Wade was killed. Jennie Wade has the sad distinction of being the only civilian killed in Gettysburg during the battle. The house, now a museum, is reputed to be haunted by Jennie's ghost.

On that fateful morning on July 12, 1863, Jennie was kneading bread dough in the kitchen; she and her mother were baking bread to give to Union soldiers. In those days, it was common practice for sharpshooters to check their aim by shooting at the doorknob on the front door. At 8:30 a.m., one Confederate marksman took aim at the doorknob on the house. Inside, Jennie was unaware of her appointment with destiny. Concentrating on the brass doorknob, the soldier slowly pulled the trigger until the gun roared and discharged a cloud of smoke. Looking at the door, he saw that he had missed his mark but hit the door. The bullet had indeed ripped through that door, then through the kitchen door and, alas, struck poor Jennie in her back shoulder and went through her body. It was a mortal wound and she fell, dying within moments.

As Donna walked by the door that had been hit by the Confederate sharpshooter, she fell to her knees from a sharp pain extending from her back to her throat. Her hands went to her throat as she began to choke,

The Mount Hope Cemetery crematorium.

unable to breathe. Her friend helped her up and half dragged her away from the house. She soon recovered; the only explanation was that Jennie's ghost had allowed her to literally feel the moment when Jennie was shot.

After she told me the story of Gettysburg, I asked if her left side was still feeling warm. She said that it was. I smiled and said, "You know, the walk takes us closer to the crematorium; it's just down there to your left."

The Flag

One early evening in August 2005, a few of my friends decided to ghost hunt in Mount Hope Cemetery in Rochester, New York. There were five of us, including Ray, a gifted psychic. We rendezvoused at the old crematorium, a stone building with a very tall chimney that hinted at its true use.

It was warm and humid, and there was no breeze. The cottonwood trees were releasing their seeds, and the waning sun backlit thousands of cottony balls gently floating down in the still air.

Mount Hope is a wonderful old cemetery with unique natural features. We walked the winding roads until we came to a section with several older graves about sixty feet ahead of us. One had a small American flag next to the headstone. For some reason, I stopped and looked at the grave for a few seconds.

As I watched the flag, it began to flutter. The rest of the group stopped and watched. The flag was moving as if a light breeze was blowing on it. Not a bit of a breeze was evident, and the grass and leaves were dead still, yet the flag was moving.

Slowly, we walked closer to the flag. It continued to move in the nonexistent breeze. As we approached to about twenty-five feet, the flag straightened out as if in a strong wind for a second and then fell back, unmoving.

I looked at Ray, who was staring intently at the flag, and asked him what his impression was. "There's a little girl lying on the grave; she was playing with the flag. She came to visit her father," he said.

We stayed for a couple of minutes, taking photographs and trying to get EVPs (electronic voice phenomenon), then we moved on. The flag remained still. Ray said that the girl was tired and was lying down next to her dad.

The Photo Assignment

In 1975, Judy was in her senior year at Monroe High School. One of her teachers, Mr. Pontillo, gave her class a photo assignment to take pictures of something that interested them. Pontillo had the students team up, decide on a photo project and sign out cameras and film. Judy teamed up with her friend Gary, and they signed out two Pentax 35mm SLRs from school and several rolls each of black-and-white film.

Judy had always been fascinated with Mount Hope Cemetery, so she suggested that they take photos of the monuments. Gary thought it was a great idea, so they planned to head for the cemetery on the weekend.

Saturday morning, they met at the front gate near the crematorium, loaded the two cameras with the film and set off through the cemetery, wandering through the older sections of Mount Hope. They passed rows of obelisks and angels, silently remembering those resting below. As they walked along, each would stop to take a picture of a monument or view that interested them.

Mount Hope Cemetery view.

Though it was a warm spring morning here, there were icy cold spots that made Judy shiver. Even Gary noticed the cold spots. They walked for several hours, taking pictures among the famous of Rochester's past. Finally, their film supply was finished, and they headed home. Both looked forward to Monday, when they could develop the film and print their photographs.

During class on Monday, Judy went into the darkroom first to develop her film. After the rinse, she took it out and looked at the negatives; something about them looked very strange. There were more than just the negative images of the cemetery on the film; it looked like misty images of people also. Judy waited impatiently for her film to dry and rushed to the enlarger.

She started making prints and was amazed at the images forming in the developer tray. There were people in the pictures, and they were dressed in odd, old-fashioned clothes. When the prints were dry, Gary and Judy examined them closely.

Memorials in Mount Hope Cemetery.

The Bausch and Lomb tomb.

Some images showed people sitting on benches among the gravestones all dressed in clothing that was from the turn of the century. The images of the people were a bit blurry and not crisp like you would expect to see from a good camera.

One picture had a man walking an old bicycle with the large front wheel down the road. Another had women in long fancy dresses and wide-brimmed hats walking among the monuments. By the Ellwanger grave (joint owner of the Ellwanger and Barry Nursery) stood a soldier dressed in a uniform worn in the First World War. One of the most bizarre was a man with a mustache sitting next to the Bausch and Lomb tomb looking forlorn.

Gary developed his film as soon as he saw the strange images on his partner's film. As he unrolled the wet film from the processing reel, he peered at the negatives, and his, too, had the same sort of strange, misty images transposed on his negatives. He printed the negatives, and sure enough, his prints had similar images of people from the past. In several pictures, Judy and Gary captured the same strange specters. The one that sticks in Judy's mind most is a large man with a beard, smoking a cigar and laughing. His image was floating off the ground next to a mausoleum. Gary had taken a picture of the same mausoleum, and the same man was there, floating next to it.

Their teacher looked at the pictures and told them that it was a nice joke. He refused to believe that they were real. He took both the pictures and negatives and told Judy and Gary to redo the assignment without the "ghosts." They did reshoot, and this time there were no misty people in the pictures. Mr. Pontillo never did return the original photos or negatives. Judy did inquire at several photo stores about what could cause the misty images. While they explained why film might look misty or foggy due to moisture or light leaks and so on, no one could explain why there were images of those people.

Judy didn't print a set of pictures for herself, something she still regrets. Concerning the original pictures and negatives, well, only Mr. Pontillo knows where they are today, and my best information has it that he has joined those souls in eternal rest.

IRONDEQUOIT

The marshy swamps and ponds of what is now the town of Irondequoit provided a great source of food for the Seneca Indians. It also was a source of mosquitoes that spread illness like malaria. The Native Americans hunted and fished the area but knew enough to establish their villages far from the range of the bloodsucking insects.

In the mid-1600s, the French landed in Irondequoit. It was part of the route used by the fur trappers. The French wished to control the area for the lucrative fur trade, and in 1687 they sent an expeditionary force to destroy the Seneca. Two thousand French soldiers along with one thousand Huron warriors (the Huron were enemies of the Seneca and allies of the French) marched down to what is now Victor, New York, to an Indian town called Ganondagan. They burned the town and all the grain stored there. They murdered many of the warriors and took captive the women and children.

Irondequoit had marshes and swamps that provided a rich source of food but were also breeding grounds for insect-borne illnesses.

The Seneca would return the favor, raiding the French settlements along the Lake Ontario coast.

In the 1700s, the British fought the French for this land. Finally, the victors of the American Revolution claimed it from British hands. The settlers planted crops and eventually drained or filled in the swamps.

In 1839, the town of Irondequoit was founded. Irondequoit soon became an agricultural area, producing some of the finest apples in the world, as well as many other fruits and vegetables. Gradually, orchards were replaced with housing tracts. The part of Irondequoit called Sea Breeze became a destination for summer vacationers with the lake, amusements and resorts emerging by the late 1800s. Today, Irondequoit is a busy suburb of Rochester.

Ghost Underpants

This strange tale takes place in Irondequoit in a house on Eventide Lane. The house was built in 1964. Sadly, the daughter of the original owners was murdered in Colorado. Her parents loved her dearly and described her as a lovely, sweet girl. Those who also knew her would agree but added that she had a mischievous sense of humor at times.

Jack and Mary purchased the house several years ago. They loved the house and the area. Nothing particularly strange had ever happened until June 3, 2008.

It was a beautiful morning when Jack and Mary woke up. Mary got out of bed first and went toward the kitchen. "Jack," she called, and he sleepily walked down the stairs into the living room. Mary was holding up a pair of women's panties.

"What is this?" she asked a bit nastily.

"They're not yours?" Jack groggily responded.

She picked four more pair out of the laundry basket next to the couch. "No, they are not!" she replied sarcastically and walked into the kitchen.

Jack knew by her voice that it was not shaping up to be a peaceful morning. He had a few of his friends over the night before and thought that one of them must have played a joke on him. "Honey, it must have been one of the guys playing a joke on me," he replied hopefully.

As he walked into the kitchen, he looked at his wife. Mary was a bit on the jealous side, and from her look he knew that she did not believe him for a second. After he had called his friends and no one confessed to the prank, Jack had a feeling that he was going to be in the doghouse for a while.

Unfortunately for Jack, this was just the first of many pairs of undies that would be found throughout their home. Several weeks later, he heard a loud and angry "Ooooh!" as Mary picked a pair of panties off of the kitchen table. About every two or three weeks, the underwear would mysteriously appear for them to find in the morning.

At first, Mary thought that Jack was entertaining another woman in the house. Then they started finding them in very strange places, like under the sink, in Jack's backpack and in other nooks and crannies around the house, as well as in the open. The underwear just kept coming, and it came in various sizes.

At the time they told me this story, they had found seventeen pairs of women's underwear. While Mary is still not amused, she knows that Jack is not secretly going on panty raids in the dark of night.

One wonders if it might not be the ghost of the original owner's daughter playing mischievous prank on the new owners.

Just When You Thought it Was Safe to Take a Shower Again...

Doreen is a waitress I met a few years ago at a local restaurant. Over the years, I would run into her now and then, and we would catch up. The last time I saw her, she told me about a strange incident that happened to her in her apartment. Doreen lived in an average upstairs apartment near Culver Road with her two children.

She was running the hot water for her shower and went to check on her children. They were sleeping soundly in their room.

When she went back in the bathroom, the air was warm and steamy and the mirror misted over. She disrobed and went in the shower. The hot water felt wonderful after the day she had at work.

Finishing, she opened the shower curtain and looked at the mirror. A feeling of horror swept over her. What looked like a four-clawed hand had streaked its mark across the mirror in the warm mist.

Heart racing, she grabbed her robe and ran out of the bathroom to check on her children. They were still sleeping peacefully in their room. The apartment door was bolted. Her heart was still pounding; she went to the kitchen, grabbed a heavy cast-iron frying pan and searched the small apartment to be sure no one was hiding.

From that time on, she always felt like someone was watching when she was in the bathroom, especially when she took a shower. Several months later, she moved to another apartment with a private bath.

SEA BREEZE

Sea Breeze is located on the shore of Lake Ontario directly north of downtown Rochester. The first settlers were farmers. Much of the area near the lakeshore was orchards, and the Irondequoit area was well known even in Europe for its fine apples.

In the later 1800s, thanks to its location on Lake Ontario and the rise of the middle class, Sea Breeze became a destination for summer relaxation. Travel in those days was limited to horse, rail or ship. Sea Breeze was close and easy to reach from Rochester by carriage and was an even quicker trip when rail lines were extended. The area offered lovely spots to relax and picnic by the lake.

From the 1870s to the 1920s, Sea Breeze was a summer destination for the middle class. Accommodations ranged from posh resorts to tents. One of the first to cater to the public was the Allen House, also known as the Sea Breeze Hotel (1865). As more people traveled to Sea Breeze to enjoy the beauty of Lake Ontario, resort hotels began to spring up, as well as rail lines that serviced the area. By the late 1800s, a regular ferry service linked Sea Breeze with other port stops along the lake including Niagara Falls, Toronto and the Thousand Islands. Ferry service continued until 1949.

Many would come to enjoy the area at what is now Sea Breeze Amusement Park, the fourth-oldest amusement park in the United States. In 1879, it was called the Picnic Grove. Some may still remember Sea Breeze Park by its old name, Dreamland, from the 1940s.

The first rides were built in 1905; through the years, there were a number of rides and attractions added, including four roller coasters. Some of the most famous rides are the carousel (built in 1915, it was destroyed by fire on March 31, 1994, and has since been rebuilt) and the Jack Rabbit (built in 1920). The Jack Rabbit is the second-oldest operating wood rollercoaster in the United States. Many other attractions were built, including a huge saltwater pool (the largest in the United States), circus-style acts and band concerts, which drew vacationers there by the droves.

Today, Sea Breeze is still open and includes a water park. You can still go for a ride on the Jack Rabbit or take a spin in the rebuilt carousel. Several of the original horse seats were saved from the fire and are used in the new carousel. Some say that every so often you can see the ghost of the old owner, who loved the carousel, standing near the old horses.

During Prohibition, there were many establishments on the waterfront that catered to more adult entertainment. For those who liked a wee drop, Sea Breeze was the place to go since it was just across the lake from Canada, a country that had no such law against producing fine liquor and beer. There was no shortage of enterprising individuals smuggling the booze and beer over to the many speakeasies that sprang up all along the shore of Lake Ontario. It was said that you could not throw a stone without hitting a speakeasy or brothel back then.

The bar now called Shamrock Jacks started out as a private residence but became both a speakeasy and brothel during Prohibition. To this day, it has several hidden rooms that were sized just right to hide the cases of Canadian whiskey and girls from the authorities. The rooms are accessed by sliding part of the wall open.

When the Great Depression hit, Sea Breeze, like all of America, fell on hard times. While the community and the amusement park did survive, sadly the resort hotels and many of the other attractions of the area never reopened after the Depression era. Some were destroyed by fire or abandoned to slowly fall apart.

Sea Breeze is still a destination for thousands each summer, though it pales in comparison to its past glory.

The Fire Hose

Founded in 1908, the Sea Breeze Fire Department is over one hundred years old. During Prohibition, it was said that the one place that you could always get a drink was the firehouse. One fireman brewed up what was known as "Sea Breeze ginger ale." The current firehouse is located directly across the street from the original firehouse. They moved to the larger building to accommodate the bigger trucks and needed space for equipment.

Now the fire department is reputed to be haunted by several children and the first chief of the fire department. The chief likes to look in on his men when they are there. He stands in the doorways and peeks in from time to time.

Down in the basement is the recreation area, and one of the most enjoyed forms of recreation is poker. Late one evening, four firemen were playing a friendly game when they heard a noise from the old hose rack.

The hose rack is made of two- by four-inch lumber in which they set the old hoses; they are rolled up and stored in the rack. A rolled-up hose must be lifted in or out of the rack. Well, one coiled hose had lifted itself out of the rack and sat upright on the floor. As the four guys watched, the hose unrolled itself on the level basement floor. A few seconds later, all four firemen decided to fold their hands and quickly bid one another good night as they hurried up the stairs and out the door. The next day, the hose

Sea Breeze Fire Department, Sea Breeze, New York.

was as they had last seen it, unrolled. It was carefully rerolled and put back in the rack.

Besides children, the Sea Breeze firehouse has several adult ghosts, including one that seems to like the second-floor ladies' room. He will stop in for a peep now and then.

The second floor has a meeting hall, kitchen and, of course, bathrooms. Over the years, several women have reported seeing a pair of eyes watching them from the bathroom mirror in the ladies' room.

Is it a ghost who doesn't think women should be in a firehouse? Or perhaps just a peeping tom?

The Reunion Inn

Culver Road, the main artery that runs from Cobb's Hill right up to Sea Breeze, was originally called Woodman Road. Woodman was the name of the family who owned a farm in the area now called Sea Breeze. In the early 1800s, the Woodmans built and lived in a one-story wooden farmhouse constructed on the same fieldstone foundation on which the Reunion Inn now sits. The Erie Canal was located right next to Cobb's Hill, so produce could be brought straight down Woodman Road in wagons and loaded onto the canalboats.

Captain Samuel Bradstreet and his wife, Lavinia, bought the property in the early 1850s, and they built the current two-story brick building in 1856. Samuel was a retired captain in the army and fought in the Blackhawk Indian War in 1832; he later became the supervisor of Irondequoit. They had two children, Samuel Jr. and Susannah.

The Bradstreet home was constructed of brick, and they used an existing fieldstone foundation from the wooden farmhouse originally built by two of the Woodman family, Sylvester and Abigail. There appears to be a marker stone in the foundation. It is unknown what may be buried under the marker stone. It has been speculated that the Woodmans may have had a child who died in infancy and that they buried the child in the basement using the stone as the marker.

The house is thought to have been part of the Underground Railroad. It was a good location where escaping slaves could hide and rest while on their way to Canada and freedom.

The family cemetery was located just down the street—it's now a parking lot for Churi's, an ice cream parlor and a Thai restaurant. It served as a cemetery for both the Woodmans and Bradstreets and included their children and spouses. In the 1960s, the remains were moved to the current Irondequoit Cemetery on Culver Road. It is unknown how much of the bodies were reburied with the headstones.

Within the past few years, several psychics have visited the Reunion. They say that nine people have died here since it was built—not unreasonable, as in the 1800s many folks preferred to stay at home rather than travel to a hospital.

During Prohibition, the home was bought, and it was turned into a speakeasy. By 1934, with Prohibition lifted, it became a legal bar with apartments in the back. It has changed owners and names a few times. It is currently owned by Jim Barnash and Steve Sahs. Jim is not a believer in ghosts, but his partner Steve has had many experiences with the ghosts of the Reunion Inn.

The Reunion Inn, Sea Breeze, New York.

The ghosts have manifested themselves to Steve a number of times. The first, many years ago, was when he went down to the basement. As he stepped off the stairs, his elbow was grabbed by "bony fingers." He was startled at first; then, realizing that there was something he could not see grabbing his arm, he ran into the beer cooler and locked the door. About twenty minutes later, he dared to make a run for the first floor. When he told some of the other co-workers what had happened in the basement, another bartender confessed that something similar had happened to him. The other bartender's name was also Steve, and he also had run into the cooler for a while.

Steve (the owner) usually opens up the Reunion every morning. One bright summer morning, he was getting the cash register ready for the day. A woman's voice chimed a cheery "Good morning!" Steve replied, "Good morning to you." He turned, expecting to see a customer, and found no one there—well, no one he could see. Another time, in the basement again, Steve heard a strange noise. He turned to see an old bottle cap rolling across the floor.

The mood is different in the cellar; a darker presence seems to prefer its eerie shadowy surroundings. Staff don't like going down there if they can help it, and some swear that they have seen sinister moving shadows. One waitress who was down in the basement told me of a shadow she saw cast on one of the doors. It was the shadow of a hanged man swaying slowly back and forth. Several psychics who visited the Reunion said that the ghost in the basement was a runaway slave (one of three in the house) who had made it to the Bradstreet home but was recaptured. He was killed for running away, and his ghost went back to the last place at which he was free.

I have been to the Reunion many times, and the primary ghost is believed to be Mrs. Lavinia Bradstreet. She and her husband built the house, and she is still very attached to it. Lavinia likes to bake, and many of the staff have smelled brownies and cupcakes baking. While they serve tasty desserts, the Reunion does not bake any desserts in house.

On the first floor, the youngest slave ghost, a little girl, likes to play. She hangs around the kitchen, where an aluminum serving tray will occasionally fly off the ice maker. Once an invisible finger pinged each pot that was hanging on the wall. Once in a while, the food will move about on the prep table in the kitchen. In the bar area, some customers have felt her touch as if she is standing next to you and touching your leg as she was watching what's going on.

One early morning, the bartender had locked the side door for the night. As she turned away from the door, there was a loud thud. She thought something had crashed into the door. Unlocking the door and carefully poking her head in, she saw the white cue ball from the pool table lying in front of the door. Moments before, when she had left, the cue ball had been on the pool table several feet away. She quickly pulled the door shut, locked it and hurried to her car.

One evening several years ago, in the upstairs back dining room, two waitresses were talking when they heard the closed doors of the room open. Not looking, one said, "Come in." As they turned to see who it was, the now open doors closed by themselves.

Several customers have seen full-body apparitions, including that of a middle-aged woman. A couple was sitting down, and each saw the ghost at the same time, standing behind the other's shoulder. One busboy also saw her dancing near the stairs on the second floor; he watched her for a few seconds until she disappeared.

One of the most amusing stories comes from a waitress who had refused to believe any of the ghost stories she had heard from her fellow staff over the years. One evening, she went to the upstairs bathroom. The upstairs one had been remodeled and was nicer than the downstairs ladies' room.

She was in the bathroom when suddenly there was a knock on the door. She was surprised, as she had seen no one else up there when she had come in.

She said, "I'll be right out." Whomever it was continued to knock, and again she said, "I'll be right out." There was no reply—just more knocking on the door.

Well, the waitress became a bit annoyed and thought it might be one of the staff playing a joke on her. Figuring she would surprise whoever was knocking, she quietly went to the door and quickly pushed the door open with her body. She nearly fell down as the door swung open freely.

The knocking had stopped, but there was no one in front of the door; she looked behind it—no one there either. She searched the upstairs, and there was nobody around. It was the last time she went to the upstairs bathroom at the Reunion.

The second-floor storage room has always felt cold. My psychic friend Shelly felt the presence of the third slave. He hides in the storage room, still angry and sullen about his fate. The storage room leads to the attic and cupola, where there is a ghost of a past owner. He sits up there, taking in the view, one of the things he enjoyed when he was alive.

The Bridge

Irondequoit Bay was once known as the "Swamp of the Seneca" when the French first discovered this area in the mid-1600s. The area was settled and swamps drained, and today the bay is an important watershed and recreation area. The bay has a relatively new swing bridge across the mouth of Irondequoit Bay. It opens in the spring to allow boats to sail freely in and out of the bay and swings closed for fall and winter so cars can go from Webster to Sea Breeze.

Some believe that water seems to draw ghosts. Sea Breeze does seem to have its share of ghost stories. This is one that takes place on the bridge one winter evening.

It was a cold January evening, bleak and quiet, a perfect night to be drinking hot cocoa and staying warm by a fire. Jerry stood on the Irondequoit Swing Bridge, the cold seeping into his hands. He was too deep in thought to notice; besides, his thoughts were colder than the winter steel.

His mind went back to that fateful summer day—the day he had lost his friend. The weather was beautiful, warm and perfect for a swim. Jerry and his buddy decided that a swim after work was the ticket to cool off and relax. They were swimming far from shore when his friend began to have difficulty keeping his head above the water. Frantically, Jerry swam to his aid, but it was too late. That day changed him; he felt that he had failed his friend. The weight of guilt hung heavy on his soul. Thoughts of whether he had been closer or swam faster roiled in his mind each day.

Jerry stared at the water and reflected gloomily. The dark thoughts seemed to draw him to the railing; it was as if the cold water rushing below was calling to him, offering a sweet release from the guilt and remorse. Mesmerized, he raised his right foot to climb over the rail. Just then, a glowing female specter dressed in white appeared at his side. The sight of her brought him out of his trance. He stared at her and her long flowing hair, and she told him simply, "Do not jump." Tears welled in his eyes, and a moment later she disappeared.

Jerry looked around and then turned and walked slowly to his car—not sure of what had happened but certain that the bridge was not the answer.

BRIGHTON

In the late 1700s, Enos Stone of Lennox, Massachusetts, purchased land in what is now Brighton. The following year, his son Orringh traveled to the new land to start a farm. He selected the site for the house, carefully building it at the meeting of two Seneca Indian trails that were used by pioneers who were traveling west to start a new life in Genesee country and beyond. He cleared the land, planted crops and built a farmhouse, which had a room that he opened to the public as a tavern. The Stone Tolan house still stands on East Avenue; the former farmhouse and tavern is now a museum.

Brighton became a town in 1814. It was originally a farming community. In the early 1800s, Vermont native Gideon Cobb opened the Monroe Avenue brickyards after having discovered that the area was rich in clay and sand. Brighton soon became the brick manufacturing capital of upstate New York until 1935. Nearby Cobb's Hill was owned by Cobb, and he mined for the clay and sand used in the brick works; later the family sold it to the City of Rochester. The city built the Cobb's Hill Reservoir in 1908, where it still provides 140 million gallons of fresh water for Rochester.

Today the brick works are gone, and Brighton is more suburbia and shopping plazas than agriculture.

The Barmaid

I met my psychic friend Shelly one evening for coffee, and our conversation led to an interesting ghostly adventure. She mentioned that where she worked, lurking in the basement, was a ghost—a ghost who wanted her story told.

For a week, Shelly was being bothered by uncomfortable feelings at work. It was as if someone was close to her neck and left shoulder. The feelings were more intense when she was in the basement. In addition, every so often the scale next to her desk would bounce up and down as if an unseen hand slapped it.

She invited me to stop by and see what I could find. I use pendulums and divining rods to "talk" to ghosts and spirits. At dinner break, we would chat with the ghost. During this time, Shelly was becoming more aware of her psychic abilities and how to use them.

The building in which Shelly works was a part of the brick works back in the 1800s, near what is now Twelve Corners in Brighton, New York. It was once a heavily forested area.

We communicated with a female ghost who said her name was Miriam. Over the course of several evenings, she communicated her story to us.

Miriam was a young woman who worked as a barmaid at the inn across the street from the brick works in the mid-1800s on what is now Monroe Avenue. It was a busy place when the brick factory workers stopped by for a drink at the end of the day. She was an only child, and her family needed the extra money. She worked long hours helping to support her family, despite the fact that it was not a job that was looked on favorably by polite society. Her one real regret was that it left her little time to find a husband, as most women had done by her age. The tavern was hardly a place to meet a husband with any promise.

Besides Miriam and another barmaid, there was the innkeeper and a black busboy who also worked there. The busboy was a big, powerful young man with, large rough hands, and though he seemed respectful enough, he liked to watch her and the other barmaid when he thought no one was looking.

The inn was smoky, gritty and filled with dirty glasses and dishes as the last of the customers left about midnight. Miriam and the busboy had to clean up the bar before they were finished. She had already caught him leering at her; he quickly averted his eyes and continued working. She knew that he looked at her all the time, but tonight the way he looked was enough to make her feel slightly unsettled. Shaking the feeling off, she continued cleaning and thought how good it would feel to get home.

It was nearing one o'clock, and Miriam decided it was time to leave; she could finish the rest of the cleaning in the morning. The busboy took a break out back.

She collected her purse and wrap and then said goodnight to the owner. As she went out the door, she took a deep breath, trying to get the smell of smoke and stale beer from her head. The owner locked the door behind her, and the sound sent a chill up her spine. It was a moonless night, and the dim lantern on the inn was like an island in a black sea. Crossing the dark street, she walked past the silent brick works; her footsteps were the only sound breaking the eerie quiet. She passed rows of finished brick piled high; they reminded her of gloomy chasms.

Suddenly, an arm reached out of the shadows and pulled her in. Before she could scream, a strong hand clamped over her mouth, and she was dragged deep into the inky catacombs. Her attacker quietly growled, "Shush now missy!" She recognized the voice as the busboy from work. She tried to scream, but darkness enveloped her.

He had not meant to kill her, but she was so delicate. Frantically, the busboy thought how to hide her body and run away, far away. He dragged her deeper into the brickyard. Using his hands, he buried her deep in a pile of sand, where he hoped her body would be undiscovered for a while.

The busboy ran away and never returned; he was never called to account for his foul deed. When Miriam's body was discovered, the authorities conducted a cursory investigation and forgot it as soon as they could. After all, Miriam was just a poor barmaid.

Frightened, lonely and sad, Miriam has waited as a ghost in the area of the old brickyard for over one hundred years. She could find no one to hear her story until Shelly. After telling it to us, Shelly helped Miriam cross over to her family and friends. She is at peace now, and the scale by Shelly's desk is quiet.

GREECE

The town of Greece was formed from the town of Gates in 1822. In the War of 1812, the Genesee militia has the distinction of preventing the British from landing at Charlotte, near the mouth of the Genesee River, and seizing control of the area.

Greece also had its ties to the Underground Railroad. Though no records have been found, the Latta family was thought to be deeply involved in hiding runaway slaves in Samuel Latta's warehouse in Charlotte, where they waited to go across the lake to freedom. Charlotte was annexed by the City of Rochester in 1916.

In 1884, the section of lakefront called Ontario Beach was known as "the Coney Island of the West." In fact, from Charlotte to Manitou Beach ran a trolley line that stopped at the many resort hotels along those eight miles of shoreline.

To mention Greece and not mention Kodak's impact would be remiss. In 1891, George Eastman started the Eastman Kodak Company. Kodak would become the largest employer in the area, as well as produce products that were used around the world. Cameras and film were Kodak's best-known products, but the industrial giant also made chemicals and many other items.

In 1934, many of the area's orchards were destroyed by a severe winter and were not replanted. Industries like the Odenbach Shipbuilding Company—which built medium-sized tankers for the army in the Second World War—

and others took the place of the lost agriculture. Today, Greece is a suburb of Rochester with large housing tracts, retail business and shopping malls.

Ghost of Emily Post

Most of you remember Emily Post—she was one of the authorities on etiquette and manners for the better half of the last century. Carol bought her house in Greece about six years ago and has learned to coexist with a prim and proper spirit who may have studied Mrs. Post's writings. Originally farmland, Greece is now a popular suburb for many of the folks who work at Kodak and in other local industries.

When she first moved in, nothing out of the ordinary happened in the house. She settled in quickly and really loved the new place. After a few months, some strange things began to happen. At first, the lights and TV would turn on in the middle of the night. Carol suspected that she might not be alone in the house. She thought a ghost that played with the lights was amusing. However, something even more bizarre began happening in the silverware drawer shortly afterward.

Set in her ways, Carol liked to place the knives, forks and spoons in the silverware drawer from right to left. About one month after the lights and TV began turning on, she was surprised to find her silverware drawer rearranged. She placed the silverware back as she had it before, but the next morning it was neatly rearranged again. It seemed that Carol's way to organize the silverware was not acceptable to the ghost.

Not deterred, Carol arranges her silverware every day, and every following morning the silverware is rearranged. The forks first, then the knives and lastly spoons, just as Emily Post would have set a table. Apparently, Carol's home has a ghost with a sense of etiquette.

The Manitou

There are several roads and a beach that were named after the Manitou, the Indian spirits who watch and protect the land. Legend has it that interesting things have been seen around Manitou Beach late at night. This appealed to a group of four young college friends, two girls and two guys, who had heard about the legend. One weekend they decided to go in search of the Manitou.

They went to Captain Braddock's, a restaurant on the bay, now closed. The restaurant owner was a friend who allowed them to stay after hours and use the place as their observation base—it had large windows that looked out on the bay. It seemed like a perfect spot from which to look out on the bay area for any Manitou passing by.

The owner told them to have fun and feel free to have some snacks that he had left in the fridge for them. Things were quiet as they looked out the windows for any signs of the Manitou. As they kept their vigil, they talked about the Manitou and other ghostly legends, and an eerie feeling began to settle over them.

About midnight, one of the guys went into the kitchen to get the tray of snacks. Moments later, they heard him scream. Rushing to the kitchen, they saw the young man paralyzed with fear looking out the window over the sink. Something was banging aggressively against the glass and then stopped suddenly. All at once, it was unnaturally quiet as they rushed to the window to see what was out there.

Whatever he had seen was gone save for distinct scratches on the glass and window frame. The young man was cold, pale and breathing heavily as they helped him to the front room and sat him down.

One of the girls gave him a glass of water, and he mumbled: "I'm OK, OK." He began to tell them what had happened. He had gone to wash his hands when in the window was a huge dark thing. "It just stood there covered in long stringy hair; looking at me with glowing red eyes. I must have screamed then," he said. "It snarled…God, its teeth…then it slashed its clawed hand across the window. Then the thing banged on the window and that's when you guys came in."

By then, the group was not worried about finding the Manitou; they seemed to have found them. They were worried about surviving the night. They were too frightened to go outside and get in their car so they decided to stay at the restaurant until daylight. They each picked up something with which to defend themselves should that thing get in. Huddled together, they spent a restless night jumping at every sound until the sun's golden glow cast the feeling of evil away.

They went around the building to take a look at the window. There were no footprints and the scratch marks on the glass had faded away, but the marks in the wood were still there: four claw marks from the Manitou's hand.

PART II

GENESEE COUNTRY EAST

PENFIELD

Daniel Penfield, the town's namesake, began buying land in 1775, and Penfield was incorporated in 1810. Daniel began building mills in 1800 along Irondequoit Creek by the falls. This attracted new settlers, and the area grew rapidly from there.

The town had a number of gristmills, flour mills and sawmills, as well as a clothing mill, carding mill, tannery, ashery, ironworks, slaughterhouse, cooperage, forge, distillery, soap factory and a triphammer. These mills and other industries were located on the banks of Irondequoit Creek. By the mid-1800s, agriculture overtook the declining milling industry in Penfield. The last working flour mill stopped production in 1972; it is now a restaurant called the Daisy Flour Mill on Blossom Road.

Tennis Anyone?

On Penfield Road, near the railroad bridge, sits a lovely home. Years ago, previous owners had put a tennis court in the garden. The husband and wife loved to play every chance they got. The years went by, and they passed away. The next owners wanted a bigger yard, so the tennis court was broken up and covered over. In its place they put a garden in that is there to this day.

The current owners love the garden and enjoy sitting out there with friends. One evening, a friend stopped by, and they all went out to the garden to sit. As they were talking, the owner noticed that her friend was distracted and looking out across the garden.

She asked if anything was wrong. Her friend focused back on her and said, "There are a couple of people over there, running around as if they were playing tennis." The owner looked at the area to which she had pointed but saw only the garden.

"You know we did find several pieces of old broken pavement that looked like it could have been from a tennis court. They were in the garden soil."

Kidd's Castle

Known as Kidd's Castle (though it is also called Webster Castle), this property is actually located in Penfield, not Webster. The house was built in 1938 by James Howard Kidd Jr. and his wife Elizabeth. The Kidds nicknamed it "the farm," but most neighbors called it Kidd's Castle. The "castle" sat on their seventy-acre estate on the southeast corner of Irondequoit Bay on Bay Road. It was a beautiful house with thirty-eight rooms, several fireplaces and a slate roof.

In the early 1960s, the property was given to the YMCA and actually became the Bay View YMCA for a while. It was vacant for a number of years and was the target of vandalism and arson, so much so that it became a nuisance for the police and fire department. In the early 1990s, the house was demolished and the debris buried on the site. All that is left is a corner of the original foundation that was incorporated into the current building.

While it was vacant, many ventured into the old mansion and property. Tony and a friend were two who poked around there in the months before it was torn down.

First they went down into the basement, dark and creepy, and they used their lighters to see. They found a tunnel and began to follow it. The ceiling sloped down to four feet as they walked for what seemed like forever. Then they saw a bit of light and found themselves in the forest near a small, empty house—perhaps the caretaker's residence? They both had a cold feeling in the woods and went back to explore the rest of the mansion.

As they walked around the dark, eerie rooms, they began to hear voices, yet they were alone. They were still using their lighters to light the way, and soon they noticed shadows following them, dark black shadows moving about. Finally, they walked into one room, and at the same moment both of their lighters exploded.

Startled but not injured as darkness surrounded them, Tony turned and headed for the front door, his friend close behind. They jumped into Tony's Jeep, and he tried to start the engine. It caught and died; he gunned the gas and tried again. Sputtering and bucking, the Jeep finally made it to the front gate; as soon as it passed the gate, the engine stopped its cantankerous sputtering and ran smoothly.

Tony returned several months later but the Kidd mansion had been demolished by then.

FAIRPORT

The next two stories come from Fairport, New York. Originally a swampy part of Perinton, Fairport was born when the Erie Canal came through in the early 1820s. The canal drained the swamps and allowed development. It soon became a busy canal port with the shipping of local agricultural crops and several industries, including Cobb Preserving, Deland Chemical and the Trescott Company.

Perinton was mostly agricultural—fruits, vegetables and grain were all shipped from Fairport by the canal and later in the mid-1800s by railroad. Another popular business along the canal was fur trapping.

The legend of how Fairport got its name goes back to a traveler who passed through the village in its first year. The story goes that the gentleman had a fine meal and several drinks at the tavern. In the afterglow of the delicious repast, he declared, "This is a fair port!" The name stuck, and the village port was named Fairport. Legend also has it that the man recanted his high praise the next morning because the hotel had bedbugs. He stormed out, never to return.

The Old Warehouse

Right off Main Street by the canal is Parce Avenue. There sits a long warehouse. Originally in the late 1880s, it was home of the Cox Shoe factory, which had moved from Rochester because of union issues. In 1903, the Sanitary Can Company bought the building, and in 1908, American Can set up operations there.

A good friend of mine owns one of the current businesses in the old warehouse and, when she heard I was writing this book, told me of several incidents that have occurred there.

While not discussed, most of the employees will admit that things are a little creepy in the warehouse. In the summer of 2008, my friend's oldest son was working on a job in the older section of the warehouse. It was the middle of the day, but that area always was dark and seemed cold even in the summer. Time flew by as he lost himself in what he was doing. The sound of the fire door closing brought him out of his concentration. Looking around, he saw no one and went back to work.

Next, a loud crash came from behind him; turning, he saw one of the cardboard storage boxes on the floor. It seemed to have fallen off the shelf. He picked it up and put it back. He began to feel a bit uneasy but got back into his project. A while later, another crash from behind—another box had fallen off the shelf. He checked the shelving to see if it was wobbly and put the box back.

Now he was getting distracted by every small noise in the shadowy warehouse. He heard another box moving on the shelf behind him. As he turned, the box hit the floor. He went to the office and told them what had happened. He still works at the warehouse but will not go into that old area without at least one other person.

An image of the original Cox shoe factory. *Courtesy of the* Fairport Historian.

Another time, the warehouse locks were being changed. Because the locksmith had to finish the job the next day, several professional security officers were hired to watch the warehouse overnight and keep a written log of anything that happened. The next morning, the two officers were nowhere to be found. Only their written log was left on a table.

The log had hourly entries of "all secure" until about midnight. The log entry noted that noises and footsteps were heard and that a search of the warehouse found no one. The last entry was marked two o'clock in the morning. The guards heard the sound of boots walking on the old, worn hardwood floor. They investigated and heard the sounds, again where there was no one there. The last entry was "officers are leaving the building."

The Judge, the Lawyer and the Prisoner

On Main Street in Fairport stands the village hall, built in 1906. The attached firehouse was built 1931. The firehouse moved into a new building, and the Fairport police took over the old firehouse. The village hall was remodeled in the 1980s and 1993 when an elevator was installed. The TV show *Mystic Encounters* went to the village hall, and together we found a number of interesting things there. Here are three stories from the second floor.

On the second floor is the main hall used for meetings and court. We decided to start there as our psychic Shelly said there was a judge sitting in one of the chairs on the dais, still presiding over his courtroom.

Several of the group tried to get EVPs. It is essentially recording the ghost talking or answering a question. One of our investigators, Jennifer, sat in the judge's seat and asked if the judge would "show us a sign."

Moments after she asked the question, the light in the judge's office turned on. The lights are on a motion sensor, and no one was near the office.

Next we headed into the hall and heard the elevator going. The group clustered around the elevator—almost expecting the doors to open and a glowing apparition to stroll out as the elevator stopped at the second floor. The doors did not open, but on the infrared camera an orb could be seen going into the elevator doors. Seconds later, the elevator started down to the first floor.

Shelly told us that she had the impression of a lawyer coming up the elevator with his briefcase and walking down the hall to the courtroom. He

Fairport Village Hall.

would shuffle some papers from his briefcase and then head back to the elevator and leave. It was a ritual he repeated each night, as he had done many times in life.

The group then went to the front of the building, where there was a sitting area with several chairs and stairs leading to the first floor. We did get several orbs on video in the area. Then Shelly pointed to one of the chairs. "He's sitting there," she said. "He's a prisoner waiting for the judge to pass sentence on him, and he is very, very angry." Shelly felt him threatening to push us down the stairs.

Despite the malicious desire of the prisoner, we all made it downstairs without incident. We left the ghosts of the second floor behind and headed for the first floor and basement—but that is another story.

WEBSTER

On February 6, 1840, Webster was established from the northern part of Penfield. They named Webster after the famous statesman Daniel Webster. Webster came to the area in 1837 and spoke to the farmers in what was then Northern Penfield. After that, they petitioned to become a separate town, the town of Webster.

In the land between Ridge Road and Lake Ontario, apples were grown as one of the major fruit crops. The town of Webster, New York, was known far and wide for its quality dried fruit. In the early 1900s, it was known as the dried apple capital of the world.

The fruit would be picked in the local orchards and then processed, dried and packaged in large dry houses located along the main rail line just north of Main Street. The dried fruit was shipped out by rail.

Up by the lake was the Forrest Lawn Hotel. That section was more of an upscale resort area for the local residents. Down the road from Forrest Lawn is the White House Lodge, now part of Webster Park. When it was first built in the early 1900s, it was a New York State sanitarium. In the 1930s, the state gave the property to the town, and it was eventually renovated and turned into a lodge for picnics and other gatherings at the lakeshore.

Birdie Hart

If you happen to be walking or driving along Railroad Avenue or Orchard Street in Webster, New York, on a dark night, you may catch a glimpse of Birdie Hart walking along. Many have seen her walking that same route she and Erwin took on a fateful night.

The year was 1904, and the dry houses employed many locals; one, a single young woman by the name of Birdie, worked at Hallauer & Sons. John W. Hallauer & Sons Evaporated Fruits was one of the thirty fruit companies that had dry houses located on Railroad Avenue.

Birdie had a boyfriend named Erwin Smith. There was something about Smith that some folks found odd. Birdie and Erwin had been seeing each other for a while, and though she knew he could be a bit strange at times, he treated her well enough. Erwin loved her, and while Birdie was fond of him,

One of the old buildings on Railroad Avenue in Webster.

she did not share his feelings. His unrequited love frustrated him greatly. He tried to control his temper and hide his building frustration, but it did erupt into an occasional argument between them.

Erwin and Birdie went out one cool evening. The crescent moon peeked out from the clouds. Seeking some privacy, they went out behind the Hallauer dry house and talked as they walked along the large wooden building. The air was filled with the scent of late fall with the hint of dried apples. Erwin associated that sweet apple scent with Birdie. Tonight he would ask her to marry him; this was not the first time he had proposed, but he would press her for an answer.

As they walked along, Erwin told her how much he loved her and then asked her for her answer about marrying him. Birdie had put him off before but felt that it was time to tell him that although she was fond of him, she knew he was not the man she wanted to marry.

With her refusal to marry him, Erwin's demeanor changed; he became more and more frustrated. He pleaded with her to marry him. Finally, Birdie blurted out, "Erwin, I don't love you."

In that instant, his frustration became hurt and then blind anger. "You, you, don't love me?" he stammered, and with that, he raised a hand and struck Birdie on the side of her head. She fell back, striking her head on a rock; horror and panic quickly replaced his rage as he realized just what he had done.

She was limp, and he was sure he had killed her. His stomach knotted, and he kneeled down and looked at poor Birdie lying unmoving on the grass. He shuddered, frightened at the thought of what he had done, then he softly cried, "Why, why did she reject me?" At his core, Erwin was a coward, and rather than face up to his wretched deed, he desperately tried to figure what to do next. "The dry house," he thought, "hide her body in the dry house!"

Yes, he could make it appear like an accident in there. Looking around to be sure that no one had seen what had happened, he forced the side door open and carried her inside.

He placed her body into a corner near the basket rack. The dry house was filled with sweet scent of drying apples. The scent that once reminded him of Birdie now burned his senses with her rejection of him. Frantically, he pulled the wooden baskets from the rack and piled them over her along with old newspaper that had been used to line the racks. Desperate to be rid of her and that scent of apples, he struck a match and set the paper and baskets on fire in several places. As he stood looking at Birdie's funeral pyre, mesmerized by the flames that were quickly spreading, he heard a faint moan from under the burning pile. Thinking that he must be mad, for she could not be still alive, he covered his ears and ran from the building as the crackling roar of the fire drowned out her pitiful cries. Erwin disappeared into the night to make his escape.

Under the rapidly burning pile, smoke built up and heat began to reach her. Birdie's last confused thought was, "No Erwin, I don't love you. My head, why does it hurt, it's so hot…" The smoke mercifully overcame Birdie before the flames reached her.

The fire was visible through the open door and windows. Nearby neighbors saw the flames, gave the alarm and helped form a bucket brigade until the local fire company could get there. Soon they had the blaze under control and saved the building. As they cleaned out the burnt debris, they found poor Birdie's scorched body under the pile of ashes and a few charred bits and pieces of baskets. Her death and the fire were ruled murder and arson, respectively.

In the end, Erwin Smith was caught and convicted for his foul deed. It was not reported what punishment was sentenced. Poor Birdie was laid to rest, yet she is still restless. She wanders the streets near the old dry house, still looking for Erwin to tell him that she won't marry him, touching her face where he hit her and wondering why it was so hot on such a cool night.

1899 Train Wreck

There were once railroad tracks running along the shore of Lake Ontario. They linked Buffalo on the western end to the Thousand Islands on the eastern end, stopping in the towns along the way. In Webster, the RW&O (the Rome, Watertown and Ogdensburg Railroad) Forrest Lawn Station was up by the lake just a ways past the mouth of Irondequoit Bay.

One of the groups with whom I go ghost hunting, the Phantom Finders, decided to pay a visit to the station on an April evening. It was the site of a tragic train collision, and they hoped to find some ghosts of the poor souls who died in the wreck.

While no one actually saw any apparitions, the area was very active for those who are sensitive to the paranormal. My friend Shelly was surrounded by the ghosts of children. Several told her what they had seen that day. At first, Shelly thought they had died in the train wreck, but there were no small children killed in the crash. It is likely that they are attached to the area in some way—perhaps they used to vacation at the beach there.

They did sense two adult ghosts from the wreck: one was the engineer who was there because of the guilt he felt in causing the accident. The other was a passenger who had his leg severed in the crash—two victims of that horrible train wreck that took place over one hundred years ago.

It was just after six o'clock the on a warm summer morning of August 10, 1889, and the local stub train had just pulled into the station. On that fateful day, the westbound express coming in from the Thousand Islands was an hour and a half late, and the engineer was trying to make up time by going much faster than usual. Signal flags had been put out, but the Forrest Lawn Station was not one of the express train's stops, and the engineer either ignored them or didn't see the flags.

The raging express locomotive slammed into the rear of the short stub train, and its last two cars were smashed to kindling. At that point, the express steam locomotive jumped the rails. One account states that the steam locomotive exploded after it derailed. Only one of the nine passengers from the local train escaped relatively unscathed from the shattered cars. Eight others were seriously injured, dead or dying. The express passengers fared better; all but those in the first passenger car behind the locomotive were unhurt.

Fifteen passengers on the platform waiting to board the local train were spared serious injury. Soon help came from the surrounding area. The injured were sent down to Rochester City Hospital for treatment; several of the grievously injured died later at the hospital. Both engines were damaged beyond repair.

Montezuma's Revenge

This story came to me via one of my fellow ghost hunting Meetup members. They say that ghosts and other entities can attach themselves to objects. If you bring the haunted item home, you will bring the attached spirit also.

Sharon and her fiancé Todd received a clay sun god ornament from a friend who was visiting Mexico. It was a strange-looking clay sculpture with feathers and a very Aztec nose. Todd liked it very much and hung it on his apartment's living room wall.

When he was home, he noticed that the lights would occasionally flicker on and off. He thought little of it, as bigger things were on his mind. He was going to marry Sharon soon and build a house in Webster, New York, on Gravel Road.

Sharon and Todd got married and built their house. The things in his old apartment were packed in boxes and shipped to the new house. It was several months before the boxes were unpacked. The sun god was put on the new family room wall.

After a few days of the idol hanging on the wall, Todd started feeling ill. Nothing really serious or life-threatening, just feeling drained, with headaches one after the other and no reprieve. Other things began happening as well, strange things.

The lights in the family room flickered while they sat and watched TV. Doors that they had left closed were wide open when they went back into the room and open doors would slam shut. To add to this, both Sharon and Todd began to feel that they were being watched, especially in the family room.

Then one day, while Sharon was vacuuming, she looked at the kitchen doorway, and standing there was a hazy, dark shadow with broad shoulders silently watching her. Startled, she dropped the vacuum hose, and the vision vanished. When Todd returned home from work that day, she told him about the shadow that was watching her. His face paled a bit, and he said, "I didn't want to scare you, but I saw a shadow figure, too—in the basement a couple of weeks ago."

They decided that they would ask a friend who was a pastor to come in and bless the house. It was a stressful time waiting for the pastor to arrive. Every so often, one of them would catch the shadow out of the corner of their eye, watching them.

When the pastor arrived, he started in the attic of the house. He carefully looked in each room, saying prayers and shutting the door when he was finished. When he got to the family room, he was immediately drawn to the sun god. He told the couple that the sculpture was the source of the problems, and he asked permission to break it.

Without hesitation, they said "Yes."

They brought him a hammer. He laid the sculpture on the coffee table and wrapped it in a thick cloth so no pieces would escape. Raising the hammer, he whispered a prayer. He struck the idol, and it screamed as it shattered. They heard footsteps, and then the outside door slammed shut. They were all a bit shaken. The atmosphere in the house felt different, as if a weight had been lifted from them.

"Is it gone?" the wife asked. The pastor nodded and took the sun god's shattered remains and told them he would dispose of it. Later that day, the pastor called and told them of his strange ride with the smashed idol.

The pastor tied the cloth up and then put the wrapped pieces on the passenger seat of his car and drove away. He had not driven far when he began to feel queasy. Soon he felt very warm, and his throat began to close— as if unseen hands were slowly choking him. Glancing at the remains, he was shocked to see the dark shadow next to him. It was staring at him, its eyes glowing a dark, angry red.

The car, too, seemed to be fighting him, and it became more difficult to steer. The car weaved back and forth, and the pastor fought with all his strength to control it as he gasped for air. He was able to slow down and pull the car into a plaza on Ridge Road. Stopping by a dumpster, he grabbed the cloth containing the idol and struggled out of the car; he threw the bundle of pieces into the dumpster.

As soon as he threw it, the invisible hands let go of his throat. Falling to his knees, the pastor took deep breaths and rubbed his neck while saying a silent prayer of thanks. Soon the evil thing would be buried in a landfill, he thought, and he prayed that it would bother no one else again.

Back at the house, Todd was already feeling better. In a couple of days, the mysterious symptoms that had been plaguing him were completely gone.

The house is now quiet. Sharon is now interested in ghost hunting. And Todd, well, he learned a new meaning for "Montezuma's Revenge."

Man with the Mustache

On Bay Road in Webster sits an old farmhouse; it was built in 1834. In the 1990s, Jackie was a young girl living there with her family.

She would occasionally see a man with a handlebar mustache watching her in the upstairs hallway. He would just stand quietly at the end of the hall, watching her as she walked to her room. Jackie had told her parents, but they had never seen him. After a while, she got used to seeing him in the hall and just accepted him as part of the old house.

Several years ago, her parents began remodeling the kitchen. They tore the floor up, and as in many old homes, there was a layer of old newspapers under the old linoleum. In with the old papers was an old photograph: a man with a handlebar mustache.

Jackie's mom showed the picture to her, saying, "We found this photograph under the old flooring. Do you recall the man you always saw upstairs? The mustache reminded me." Jackie looked at it and said, "Oh my God! That's the man who used to watch me in the hall."

PART III

GENESEE COUNTRY WEST

CHILI

Originally part of the hunting ground of the Seneca Indians, the area that would become Chili was forested and had abundant game. The Chili area was first settled by Revolutionary War veteran Captain Joseph Morgan in 1792. One must admire the measure of a man who stands in the wilderness and sees not only a homestead but also a community—one that can be built with but a few simple tools, an ox or horse and little else. Put most modern men in the same spot, and they would probably be looking for the nearest fast-food restaurant.

Chili officially split from the town of Riga in 1822. The first business to spring up was Stephen Peabody's distillery; an amusing side note to this is that North Chili was a dry town for almost one hundred years due to the temperance movement. Other businesses followed, including a sawmill and gristmill. The forests were cut to clear the land to plant crops and for lumber with which to build homes for the growing number of settlers coming into the area. After the timber was cut, Chili primarily became an agricultural town, growing crops and raising livestock.

North Chili was home to many Free Methodists, one of the religions started in Genesee country. Not only did they believe in temperance, but they were also staunch abolitionists. Many of those in North Chili were involved in the Underground Railroad.

One of the more interesting characters who frequented Chili was old Frog Leg George. Now at the turn of the century, frog legs were a popular food, sort of like chicken wings are today, and Frog Leg George was the entrepreneur who supplied most of the amphibian's lower limbs to local restaurants. He would hunt them in the marshes and swamps of the area and deliver them in his dilapidated buggy pulled by a mule. It was hard to miss George, roughly dressed and driving his buggy loaded with freshly caught frog legs rattling down the road. He lived to see the age of the horseless carriage and would grumble and cuss at the newfangled automobiles that would pass him.

There are two theories as to why the town was called Chili (pronounced with two long *i*'s at the end). The first is that Chili was named after the country Chile in South America. The other is that it is a derivative of Chiliast or Chilian, the religion of some of the early settlers out of Pennsylvania. Today, Chili is a growing suburb, though it still has a thriving agricultural community.

Till Death Do Us Part…or Maybe Not

This story takes place a few years back in Chili. Today, Chili is a small town, a suburb with restaurants and shopping. On one of the small roads off the beaten path lived a couple. The wife was not a happy woman. She made sure that her husband, John, knew that she was miserable. She also was very jealous of her husband and wanted him home all the time unless he was working.

One day, when John returned home from work, he found his wife lying dead on the floor. While sad, it was in a way a relief for him, and after the funeral he felt much of the stress go away. He was an easygoing guy and was content to leave the house just as it was, including her favorite chair, which he never sat in.

After a year, he began dating a woman named June. For some reason, she would always feel cold when she visited John at his home. John never felt chilly in the house but would turn the thermostat up for her. Even then, June still felt chilled.

After they had been dating for a while, another unusual thing began to happen. Every once in a while, John would find the picture of his deceased wife knocked over the morning after June had visited. Sometimes it was even on the floor. He just thought it was the cat, but it was on a shelf upon which that the cat never jumped, and more interestingly, it had never happened before he started dating June, nor did the cat knock over any of the other pictures on the shelf.

When John had a short business trip to go on for work, he asked June to housesit. Besides the cat, he also had a dog, and it would be easier for June to let Rover out and feed both animals if she stayed over. June had never felt really comfortable in the house, but she agreed to stay at the house while John was gone.

The first night, she watched some TV and then took the dog out for a bit. She locked the house up and got ready for bed. June made sure that the animals were out of the bedroom and shut the door. Waking up in the morning, she didn't feel rested and refreshed. As she swung her legs to the floor, she noticed that her left leg was scratched. There were red scratch marks running from just below her knee to her ankle. She had no recollection of feeling her leg being scratched in the night—only a vague remembrance of an unsettling dream. June began to feel that she should have thought more carefully about housesitting.

She dressed quickly, took care of the animals and left without further incident. For the rest of her time housesitting, June did not sleep over and just quickly ran over to check the house and take care of the dog and cat. When John returned and saw the marks on her leg, he thought it was the cat. She swore that the cat was not in the bedroom that night and that her leg was fine when she went to bed.

June felt uneasy about what had happened and began to suspect that it might be more than the cat knocking over the picture and scratching her leg. She contacted my ghost hunting group, and Shelly accompanied me to John's house.

As soon as we entered, Shelly could feel a female presence. We sat in the living room, and no one chose the favorite chair of the wife. As they told us what was going on, Shelly looked over to the empty chair and said, "It's your dead wife, and she is sitting right there watching us." Shelly pointed to the empty chair.

Shelly began to tell us that the woman was unhappy that we were there, mad at her husband and just miserable. With the exception of John, she didn't like anyone in her house—especially another woman in her bed, even if John wasn't there at the time.

Apparently, John's wife decided to stay around after her death. She was still jealous of John being with another woman, as well as being just as miserable as she had been in life—perhaps proof that misery does love company, at least the company of a spouse.

GATES

Gates was originally called Northampton and then changed its name in honor of General Horatio Gates. The town was organized in 1797 and incorporated in 1813. Gates is now the smallest town in Monroe County because the town's land was annexed nine times over the years to the city of Rochester and the town of Greece.

Today, rattlesnakes are not common in the area, but in the 1800s they were one of the biggest nuisances in town. This brings us to one of the more colorful characters I mentioned earlier, a man who helped Gates and other towns with their snake problems. He arrived in Rochester in 1892 as Pete Gruber. Nicknamed Rattlesnake Pete, his signatures were a drooping mustache and a rattlesnake skin vest. At the time, there was a bounty on rattlesnakes, and Pete used to go on regular snake hunts. He would gather rattlesnakes and black snakes from Gates and other nearby areas. He had quite a collection of snakeskin clothing made from some of the less fortunate victims of the hunts. He wore his custom-made snakeskin collection every day, as well as displayed a number of live snakes in his saloon and restaurant.

For years, Rattlesnake Pete's Saloon & Museum was a fixture at 8 and 10 Mill Street in downtown Rochester. The museum had a dubious display of curios that included the first coin-operated nickelodeon piano built by Pete himself, an old cigar butt supposedly smoked by the last man to be executed at Auburn Prison, a pipe that once belonged to John Wilkes Booth and the shovel used to break the ground for the White House, among other odd exhibits, including peep shows that had pictures of nude women. One can imagine walking into his establishment and seeing curios and snakeskins decorating the walls and ceiling and a large glass tank of live snakes on the bar.

He also practiced "medicine" using the blacksnakes to cure ailments such as goiter, deafness, croup, blood poison and rheumatism by hanging them around a person's neck. The snake would coil and constrict around the patient's neck. The massaging action on a goiter might have given some temporary relief. And, of course, true to his name, he sold rattlesnake oil.

He was obsessed with snakes but also loved dogs, especially Saint Bernards. He had several of the large dogs, and he would take them for rides in his red Rambler with two brass serpent head hood ornaments. In 1901, Rattlesnake Pete nearly met his demise when he reached into a tank of one hundred rattlesnakes, and one four-foot viper bit him in an artery. Pete passed away in 1932 and is buried at Holy Sepulcher Cemetery.

Gates was part of a flourishing seed and nursery industry that started in the 1800s. The first truly successful one was Asa Rowe's Monroe Garden and Nursery in Greece, selling seeds by catalogue in 1833. There were many entrepreneurs who started successful nursery businesses in Monroe County; some like Crosman Seeds are still with us today. In Rochester, the largest seed and nursery business was the Ellwanger and Barry Nursery started in 1840; by 1871, they had 650 acres under cultivation. They donated 20 acres to the City of Rochester to create Highland Park in 1888. In 1879, Englishman Joseph Harris started the Joseph Harris Company in Gates, selling seeds. The company is still in business in Gates. The blooming nursery business helped Rochester's nickname change from the Flour City to the Flower City.

Still an agricultural area, today Gates has become more of a suburb than the rural farming community it once was.

Leave a Light On for Me

Bill was a volunteer fireman who lived in Gates on Dorstone Road just down from the fire department. He lived in an older home; however, nothing out of the ordinary happened while he owned it—that is, except for the nights the fire station's siren would go off, calling the volunteers to the station.

As a volunteer fireman, he used to be called to fires at all hours of the night. Dashing out, he never remembered to turn the lights on. On many of those nights, when he came home, the lights would be on as if welcoming him back home after a hard night's work saving lives and property.

Bill has since moved, but he always wondered who it was that kept a light on for him on those nights he answered the call.

A farm in Hilton, New York.

PARMA

Parma was created in 1808 and named after Parma in Italy. The first order of business was to vote on building a pound for stray animals—not the dogs and

cats we think of today that are rounded up by the local dogcatcher but rather the wayward cow, horse or other livestock that may have strayed from their farm.

Parma extends to the lakeshore, where on a point of land jutting into of Lake Ontario sits a ninety-seven-foot-high brick lighthouse. The point is called Bogus Point, an odd name for sure. Rumor has it that this was the spot from which counterfeit money was smuggled back and forth to Canada. There was a secret cave in which they stashed the counterfeit money (just like the tunnels rumored to be under Mount Hope Cemetery). The lighthouse was commissioned in 1895 when Inspector Charles Gridley approved it for use as the brightest light on Lake Ontario.

At the southern end of Parma is Hinckleyville, named after Baptist parson, the Reverend Jonathan Hinckley. Reverend Hinckley had a bit of a rascal in him. You see, the good parson had a mill, and in his spare time, he would make some of the best grain whiskey in the area. One must wonder if the old adage "idle hands are the devil's workshop" crossed the minds of more than one churchgoing soul.

The Wagon

It was a cold, snowy day. Beth was driving home in her Ford Escort on Route 259 by Parma Corners. The road took a dip, and there was a culvert at the bottom to keep the road from flooding when it rained. She looked ahead and panicked—what seemed like a large moving van was at an angle, blocking the road.

She began pumping her brakes, but the slick pavement was just making her car fishtail. Though slowing, there was no way she would stop in time. Bracing for impact, she held her breath. Her car slid closer; she realized the van was really a wagon, a wooden wagon. She could make out the canvas and wood planks. It was unreal as her car "hit" the wagon, for her car slowly passed right through it and stopped about twenty feet past it.

When Beth got out of her car to look, the wagon was gone. For a moment, she could feel an intense pain and loss coming from the area. The feeling slowly faded. She drove home, trying to make sense of what she had seen and felt.

Slavery had been abolished in New York State. The Fugitive Slave Act (1850) did allow runaway slaves to be hunted and recaptured, with a bounty for each caught. This allowed what amounted to federal marshals and legal bounty hunters patrolling the network of routes known as the Underground Railroad taken by fleeing slaves. New York reputedly had many citizens who helped slaves to escape, despite the fines and jail time for anyone caught helping a runaway. Those who helped the runaway slaves along on the Underground Railroad routes were called conductors.

This ghost story starts with two slave families running for freedom in Parma, New York. Apples were the primary agricultural crop at the time. In Parma, the local Underground Railroad stations would sometimes use freight wagons to hide the runaways. This stop on the journey to freedom was run by free black businessman Walter Vond, who owned the local dry goods store. He would bring them to Lake Ontario, where the runaways would be put on boats headed for Canada and freedom.

It was a cold, rainy day in the mid-1800s. Two freight wagons pulled up to Parma Corners. They were loaded with dry goods for delivery. Two men in oilskin coats blocked the road. Their badges told the two men on the wagons that they were bounty hunters looking for runaway slaves. The horses snorted and stopped, and the rain beat on the canvas tarps covering the wagons.

The owner of the wagons was in the lead; he was well-known local black businessman Walter Vond. The second wagon was driven by another black man.

"Steady," said Vond to his wagon team. "What can I do for you?" he asked the two men.

"We are looking for several fugitive slaves we heard were in the area," the taller of the two said.

Vond replied, "I own the dry goods store in town, and this is my hired hand."

"We know who you are," the tall one said with disdain. The bounty hunters began to walk to the back of the second wagon.

The black man on the second wagon pulled his old hat a bit lower and quietly watched the two men. His heart raced as he hid his anxiety from the bounty hunters.

Vond looked back at the driver on the second wagon and said, "We have a big load here to deliver, and I don't want to get it all wet while you are around looking. My customers won't like it." Ignoring him, one of the men went to the back gate of the wagon and lifted the canvas up.

His eyes opened wide as he saw three frightened faces looking at him. He was about to yell for his partner when the driver jumped off the wagon and tackled the man. The other bounty hunter ran to help, and the three men rolled in the mud, exchanging blows.

Mr. Vond shouted, "Come to this wagon!" and from under the other wagon's tarp a woman and two children scampered out. They moved slowly at first, both scared and not wanting to leave their husband and father. The woman lifted the two children into Vond's wagon.

One of the bounty hunters, seeing them, got up and lunged at the three getting on the first wagon. The man managed to grab the woman's legs and dress just as she was climbing on the wagon. Vond laid on the whip, and the wagon tore away.

For a few seconds, the woman desperately hung on to the wagon as it dragged both her and the bounty hunter behind it. Her strength was ebbing, and despite her friend's hands trying to pull her in, she slipped, pulled away by the bounty hunter. They lay in the mud as Walter Vond's wagon pulled quickly away. They got up, and the bounty man grabbed her arm.

Her husband had knocked the wind out of the other bounty man and climbed back on the wagon. He started it straight for the bounty hunter, who was struggling with his wife. The bounty hunter leaped back and released the woman as the horses brushed him. Slowing slightly, the man reached down, grabbed his wife and pulled her up into the wagon. He laid on the reins, and the wagon sped up, turning on Hilton Parma Corners Road. The two bounty hunters raced to their horses and soon were in fast pursuit.

Vond's wagon was far ahead, lost in the heavy rain. The man and his wife were not so lucky; they looked back and saw the bounty hunters gaining on their wagon. He frantically urged on the horses faster. The wagon slid to and fro on the slippery, muddy road. The road ahead was hard to see in the rain and mist; it dipped at the bottom of a hill, and there was a flood washing out the road from the downpour.

Too late to stop, the horses slowed, but the loaded wagon hit the water and jackknifed, throwing the man and woman into the water. They were swept away in the cold, fast current. Battered from the fall and hit by debris washed in the freezing torrent, she lost consciousness. As darkness overcame her, she thought of their children and knew that Walter had enough time to get them away to safety. Her husband was desperately trying to get to her, but the heavy, wet clothing and freezing water was dragging him under. With his last ounce of strength, he reached out for her, and then his body, now lifeless, was carried downstream by the current.

When the two bounty hunters came to the wagon, they jumped down from their mounts and with sour expressions watched the bodies wash down the gully in the flood. They had lost the first wagon and knew that it was going to take time to recover the bodies from this one.

If you are on Route 259 near Parma in bad weather, slow down. You might just see a wagon blocking the road. If you do, say a prayer for those who died trying to live free.

Man in Black

Mary's boyfriend lived in Hilton, a small village west of Rochester in the town of Parma. It was named after a beloved minister and Civil War veteran named Reverend Charles Hilton. Although Hilton is known for apple orchards and named for a man of God, there are perhaps darker things that also dwell there.

Every time Mary was in her boyfriend's house, several areas would feel cold and despondent, most strongly the master bedroom and stairway. While the feelings bothered her, she did her best to ignore them. The feelings had nothing to do with her boyfriend Todd; they seemed to be attached to the house.

Suppressing the feelings worked for a while, until she began to be aware of something watching her. The eerie sensations were worst in the stairway. Then one evening when she was over for a visit, there by the stairs was a man, dressed in black and leaning against the wall. His arms were crossed and he was scowling at her. The way he looked at Mary sent shivers down her spine. She called Todd in and pointed at the dark specter, but he saw nothing.

Then, faintly, she could hear a woman crying from upstairs. Mary followed the sobbing to the master bedroom. In the room she saw the ghost of a young woman lying on the bed, crying. When Mary walked closer, the ghost looked at her and pleaded for Mary's help to escape. The sobbing ghost told her that the man in black keeps her locked away in the bedroom, abusing her for his carnal desires.

Hilton, New York apple and corn crops.

It had begun so long ago in the early 1800s. He was a wealthy landowner who had had just settled in Hilton. He met her on a business trip to New England and was smitten by her beauty. He had convinced her to come for a visit to see his new property.

At first, he seemed quite nice, but soon he showed his true nature. He was an avaricious, controlling and heartless man. His real personality repulsed and even frightened her. She told him that she was not interested and would be going back to New England immediately.

At that, his eyes filled with rage, and he said, "You will not be leaving, my dear."

He roughly led her to the upstairs bedroom and locked her in. He treated her as a slave, for his dark soul desired only submission to his will.

She was a prisoner in his home; weeks dragged into months. She tried to resist him, but he forced himself violently upon her. Desperate and despondent, she could not go on.

One evening, she sat on the bed holding a pair of sewing scissors in her hands. For a long while she stared at them. Hearing a noise—his footsteps on the stairs—she raised the scissors to her breast. He opened the door, and as she looked at the face she hated so, she smiled and fell to the floor face down. The scissors were driven deep in her breast. He rushed to her and clutched her head in his hands and looked deep into her dying eyes.

Blood trickled from her mouth as she softly said, "I am free…"

As the cold darkness closed around her, the last words she heard was his angry curse: "Death will not free you from me!"

Mary felt sorry for the ghostly lady. She continued to see Todd for a while, though she began to avoid going over to his house because the ghost of the man in black made her too uncomfortable.

As for the poor despondent ghost lady, in life the man in black possessed her body, but in death he possessed her soul. So if you should be in a house in Hilton and see the ghostly figure of a man in black, listen carefully, for you may hear the sound of a crying woman coming from upstairs.

ALBION

Albion was formed in 1825 as a largely agricultural community. When the Barge Canal ran through the town, it spurred other industry and helped to grow the town. By 1860, there were thirty-eight sawmills to support the timber industry, and three tanneries were in operation to process hides into leather. The early settlers found the soil to be very productive.

Directly below the rich soil was a layer of Medina sandstone, which gave rise to many sandstone quarries. The stone was widely used for the

Orleans County Courthouse, circa 1857–58 in Albion.

Erie Canal walls, bridges and building foundations. There are some fine examples of Medina sandstone buildings including the Pullman Universalist Church and the First Presbyterian Church. It was a major industry in the area until the 1920s, when bad management and labor problems along with competition from Vermont granite closed the quarries. The old quarries are still visible today.

Albion became the county seat of Orleans County and also the shipping center for the area. The major products were wheat, lumber, potash and pork. By the 1840s, horses and livestock were also big businesses in the Albion area.

The canal was Albion's main transportation link until the railroad came in 1852; this was the beginning of the end for the passenger canal packets. In the 1880s, the railroad became the main freight carrier, and crop storage and processing businesses (fruit evapories, grain and bean elevators, vinegar works and cold storages) grew up along the railroad. Then, in 1903, the Burt Olney Canning Factory, specializing in tomatoes, peas, beans and corn, was constructed. This company eventually merged with General Foods during World War II, becoming Birdseye Snider (complete with a research laboratory for frozen foods) and then Hunt Wesson. The Lipton plant was established in the Thomas J. Sweet Canning factory in 1942 to provide dried food for the military. These two plants became the main industries in Albion, which suffered when Hunt Wesson closed in 1970 and Lipton in 1980.

The Albion Stomp

A gentleman named Don shared this story with me. He grew up in the small town of Albion, a bit west of Rochester, in a house that had a rather noisy ghost.

On County House Road in Albion sits an old farmhouse. Herb and Carol bought the house in the 1960s. They felt that the country was a wonderful place in which to raise their four children, Don, Herb, Pat and Beverly. Don was about five when they moved in.

Things did not feel right from the start. They all heard noises that could not be accounted for. Every time a banging noise came from the basement, Don's father would go down to see what was making the noise. Every time he would find nothing. Finally, Carol asked the parish priest to come and bless the house, hoping that a blessing would put an end to the strange sounds.

The local parish priest came over, and as the family watched, he began to bless the home. Almost as soon as he entered the house, the priest became very nervous. He went right to the kitchen and rapidly recited a prayer in a stressed voice. Out of his pocket he drew a small bottle of holy water and quickly sprayed it in several directions. Turning to the family he told them he had other calls to make and hurried out of the house.

That night, after the children were sent to bed, the parents heard loud banging noises coming from the walls, much worse than before. From the floor came a noise like someone pounding a broomstick against the floor from the cellar. The father went down the cellar stairs and stood directly under the spot the noise was coming from. He could see nothing. As he looked at where the sound was coming from, he felt a dark coldness envelop him. After a while, the banging finally stopped.

Things settled down a bit after that, but on most nights noises could be heard. Don would lie in bed and hear footsteps, boots with spurs, stomping up the stairs and down the hall. His two brothers and sister heard them also. After a while, they got used to the nightly routine.

A few years later, Don was in his first year of college, and he had returned home for Christmas break. The rest of the family was out that evening, and Don was relaxing on the couch watching TV; the family dog was curled up by his feet. From the wall behind him came a banging noise; the dog lifted his head and looked toward the wall. Don tried to rationalize the noise: a water pipe or the furnace. The banging became louder and louder. It started to come from directly behind Don's head. He searched downstairs, looking for what could be making the noise. Finding nothing, he sat back down and was determined to figure out what was causing this. He thought someone must be in the house trying to scare him. Then the banging began to come from the floor, like a broomstick hitting the floor. It was so hard that Don's feet started to bounce up and down.

The phone rang, and as he got up to answer it, from behind he heard footsteps walking toward him from the next room. He looked toward the sound only to see the dog headed straight for the front door in the kitchen. Answering the phone, it was Don's brother, Herb, and when he told him what was going on his brother said that he would be right home and for Don to get out of the house. Don hung up and went to the kitchen, where the dog was pawing at the door; he turned toward the living room and heard loud stomping footsteps rushing straight for him. Grabbing his keys, he ran out the door with the dog.

Don headed across the street to the neighbors; his heart was racing and he was a bit pale. He told them that there may be someone in the house. The husband grabbed a gun, and he went back over with Don. All was quiet as they entered the house; they searched from basement to attic but found nothing. When Don's parents got back, he told them what had happened. They did not look surprised. His mom said that those noises happened every once in a while—usually later at night when the children were asleep and only she and their dad were awake.

Later, when Don went up to bed, he immediately felt a presence. Looking at his bed, he noticed there was a depression on the blanket; it was shaped like a man lying down. He looked at it, and his feelings of fear turned to anger. He said in a shaky voice, "This is my room. This is my parents' house. Go back to hell where you came from!" From then on, Don was not bothered again.

The family eventually came to accept their noisy phantom and nicknamed him Oscar. The couple still own the house; their four children are grown and off on their own. While it has become much quieter, now and then a strange noise is heard. Herb or Carol will say, "There's Oscar at it again."

Hey, Move Over! I Want to Watch TV, Too!

In a little two-story house near the canal in Albion lives a woman named Lyn. Through the years, Lyn has seen many of her family pass on, including her father and brother. Though Lyn does have the gift of being able to sense ghosts, she keeps it to herself for the most part.

When her children were young, she would often see her father coming to visit and play with his grandchildren. The children were seemingly oblivious to the fact that it was grandpa's spirit and that he was not physically there with them.

Her brother was a bit more mischievous than dad. If he was in a playful mood, Lyn could not lay out a pair of socks without one disappearing when she turned her back. Hiding the keys was another frequent prank. Occasionally, Lyn would do something that she knew would upset them and usually had to endure an evening of pictures flying off the wall.

One time, Lyn's friend, Will, was staying over for several days. Lyn thought he was acting a bit strange the first day he was there. The second evening she had to go out for a while. When she returned, the TV was on in the living room, but Will was not in there. She looked in the kitchen, and he was standing there with a peculiar, pale look on his face.

Lyn's house in Albion.

Lyn asked, "Is something wrong?"

Will looked at her and replied, "Well, I didn't want to say anything this morning, but last night I saw someone in the dining room when I got up."

"Who was it?" Lyn asked.

"I don't know. She disappeared a moment after I saw her, but then tonight…" Will said.

Lyn was beginning to smile but tried to look concerned. "What about tonight?"

"Well, I got up to get a drink, and when I went back to watch TV there was a man and a woman sitting on the couch. They looked at me and then went back to watching TV. I wasn't about to sit next to them, so I came back into the kitchen," he said.

By this time, Lyn was smiling, and Will asked suspiciously, "You know this place is haunted, don't you?"

In between chuckles, Lyn told him about the family ghosts that she has seen. "Yes, it sounds like you saw my brother, and the woman, I think, is my aunt."

Lyn told him of some of the happenings around the house, and they talked about it for several hours. Will is still a good friend, and though he still visits, he refuses to stay overnight anymore.

Last Embrace

Jackie and George lived in Albion, New York. Now Albion is a rural community with lots of farms and open spaces. George loved to hunt, and on one fateful, crisp November morning several years ago, he went out to go deer hunting. He was looking forward to getting a nice buck and stocking the freezer with venison.

He drove down a lonely road to a small dirt path that led into the woods. Parking on the shoulder, he got out and began to put on his coat and orange vest. He heard a noise, looked up the road and saw another car coming down the road. It pulled up behind his, and a scruffy young man got out and said, "Can you help me?" George looked at him as he got out and stood by the car. A bad feeling churned in the pit of his stomach, and he began to walk toward the trunk, where his shotgun was locked up. The man blocked him from the trunk, grabbed his collar with his left hand and pressed a long, thin knife to his throat. "Let's take a little walk in the woods buddy," he slurred, his breath reeking of beer. He pushed George toward the dirt path. George began to run, hoping he could get away or maybe grab a branch to fend him off if he followed.

The young man cursed and began to run after him. George ran into the woods with the man close behind him. He saw a good-sized branch, slowing down he reached for it. Just as his hand grasped it, the younger man jumped on his back and knocked him down. Pain and then darkness closed in. He was in another place, his home, and his wife was walking up the stairs. He walked up and embraced her, whispering, "I love you." Somehow, he knew he could not stay, and as the room faded, a bright light enveloped him.

Jackie was walking up the stairs when she stopped for a moment. She felt strong arms around her—they were George's arms—and thought she heard him whisper in her ear. A feeling of loss hit her, and she sat down on the stairs for a moment. She began to cry and worry about George but then rationalized that it was silly; he would be home in a few hours. She busied herself with dinner and waited, praying to hear the sound of the side door.

Dinner had gotten cold, and Jackie could wait no longer. She called the county sheriff's office and told them that her husband was missing. The sheriff assured her they would look for him.

It was a restless night of worry. Finally, the next day the sheriff called. It was the worst news. Deputies found George's body. It had been hidden off the path in the woods. The murderer was caught shortly after they found George's body.

When they told Jackie the estimated time he had died, she collapsed into a nearby chair. It was about the same time she had felt him embrace her on the stairs. George had paid a visit to his wife for a last goodbye.

BATAVIA

In 1802, Joseph Ellicott established the Holland Land Office in what is now Batavia. The office sold parcels of land from the company's Holland purchase, which included 3.5 million acres of land extending from Lake Erie past Batavia and from Lake Ontario south to Pennsylvania. The expression "doing a land office business" comes from the Holland Land Office. Some days, the line of people ready to buy land was out the door. Elliot was also the first to standardize the twelve-inch ruler by taking the average of what was then used as one-foot ruler. He then used this standard rule to survey western New York. He included his brass standard ruler with each of his surveyor's field books.

Batavia became the county seat of Genesee County and, in 1915, was incorporated into a city. While bypassed by the Erie Canal, both roads and railroads went through Batavia and allowed it to grow as both an agricultural and industrial center. Batavia's economy bustled with the manufacturing of tractors, agricultural equipment, shoes and more, including a center for tool and die shops.

The Empty Room

Years ago, Sue worked at the Batavia Nursing Home. It was and still is a fine facility for geriatric care, and she enjoyed working there. As at many nursing homes, there are stories that are only whispered among the staff. Nurses from several area nursing homes have told me about shadowy figures visiting the rooms—perhaps the last one in which they had stayed. At another, built on the site of a school that had burned down, children can be heard playing. Every now and then, one of the residents will tell the children to quiet down.

At the nursing home at which Sue worked, there was one room usually kept vacant; the staff gave it a wide berth if possible. It looks like any of the other rooms, but looks can be deceiving. The corridor outside the room is cold no matter what the thermostat read. Some nights, the room's light would turn on, or the privacy curtains would open even though there was no one in it. Stranger still are the moving shadows that are seen near the door and through the window.

The room was occasionally used, but it has never had a long-term resident. It seems that most patients who have been given that room—no matter the age or affliction—usually pass away within two to three months. It seems that the room prefers to stay empty.

May I Have a Ride?

This ghost story is a classic; you can find many similar ones from all parts of the world. It is known as the "vanishing hitchhiker" story, but the woman who told it to me swears that it happened to her.

The events in this story took place several years ago for a young woman named Debbie, who lives in the small town of Basom, west of Rochester. It was a Wednesday, and like most Wednesdays, Debbie was shopping at the Tops grocery store in Batavia, New York. From out of nowhere, an older woman walked up to her and asked, "My name is Kate, and I hate to bother you, but could you please give me a ride?" The woman seemed very nice. Kate explained that she had just come in on the bus, her daughter was not here to pick her up and she had no way to get to her daughter's.

The first thought that struck Debbie was: of all the other people in the store, why ask her? Then she wondered why the woman had come all the way to Tops for a ride when the bus stop was in another part of town. She remembered that it used to be located just across the street about two years earlier before the bus company had moved it across town.

Debbie felt sorry for the woman and agreed to drive her. When asked where her daughter lived, Kate replied "Lewiston Road in Oakfield," a nearby town. Surprised, Debbie replied that she knew where the road was because she used to live there as a child. As they drove along, the women reminisced about the area. They turned onto the road, and soon Kate pointed to her daughter's house. "No!" Debbie exclaimed; her heart skipped a beat. "That's the house I used to live in."

Upon hearing that, Kate smiled and insisted that she must come in for a visit. They pulled in the driveway, and Kate went into the house. Debbie followed.

When Debbie walked into the room, the older woman was nowhere to be seen. On the floor was a young boy, perhaps two years old, smiling and laughing. She wondered where the older woman went; a moment later, a woman's voice came out of another room: "You are always so happy on Wednesdays." The child's mother came out of another room, looked at her strangely and said, "Who are you and what are you doing in my house?"

A bit mystified, Debbie told her who she was and explained that she gave an older woman a ride here from the Batavia Tops because no one was there to pick her up. She also explained how surprised she was because she used to live here as a child. Puzzled, the mom said that there was no one else here. Debbie described the lady, walked to a photograph hanging on the wall and said, "This is her; she said her name was Kate."

The young mother's hands went up to her mouth, and her face went pale. "That's my mother. She used to take the bus from Buffalo almost every Wednesday to visit here, and I would pick her up at the old bus stop across from the Tops grocery store in Batavia. She passed away two years ago, about the time they moved the old bus stop."

The two women stared at each other not knowing what to say. The boy ignored them and was chatting happily away as he did every Wednesday when Grandma stopped by to visit.

The Ouija Board of Captain Kidd

Arrrgh matey! Were there pirates in Genesee country? Well, not that I could find, but legend has it that Sylvester Woodman moved to Sea Breeze from the East Coast because of his association with pirates. There is no evidence in the records to substantiate Mr. Woodsman having anything to do with pirates. History is clear; pirates did plunder up and down the East Coast. Captain Kidd reputedly hid treasure as far north as the famous money pit on Oak Island, Nova Scotia, and Block Island off the north end of Long Island. Some of Kidd's buried treasure was recovered from Gardiners Island in 1699, a small island off the north coast of Long Island.

The next part of this story involves a Ouija board—the "talking board" believed to divine answers from the "spirits." Those seated around the board would lightly touch the planchette, and it would move around, spelling out the answer. There are a number of beautiful boards, some hand crafted and others mass produced; many have become collector's items. Who invented the Ouija board is unknown, though the first patent for the modern-style Ouija board was awarded in 1891 to Charles Kennard.

The Ouija board has acquired a dangerous and even evil reputation for attracting bad entities. Even today, some people will not even enter a room with a Ouija board in it. Many people have had strange experiences when using the board.

How can we tie pirates and Ouija boards together? Well, a lady named Ann told me about her and her friends' first and last encounter with a Ouija board, and you may have guessed who they were trying to contact, ye landlubber.

When Ann was young, she was fascinated with pirates. Back then, there were no video games, and children loved to play using their imagination. Ann's favorite game was playing pirate. Their neighborhood became the high seas, where they sailed from one adventure to another, swords swinging, peg legs clacking on the deck, eye patches present—Aaargh!—and the most important thing: the search for pirate's treasure!

Ann fondly recalled those days when she was a young girl; she and her friends would play pirate every chance they could. Each day they sailed far and wide in their backyards, looking for buried treasure. If only they had a real pirate treasure map marked with an X (apparently the ones they made from notebook paper and crayons were not as accurate in marking where those gold doubloons lay buried as they had hoped).

Now where to find a real treasure map? They had searched and found no pirates, living or otherwise, in the neighborhood. Likewise, they had dug a lot of holes looking for treasure; no maps had they found in any of them. Even in the library where there were so many stories of pirates and their treasure, none had ever mentioned western New York State as the preferred spot to bury treasure!

One day, Ann and her friends found an old Ouija board in a heap of discarded items by the curb. A real Ouija board to talk to spirits—their minds raced with thoughts of the ways they could use it! They could forget the crayon maps, contact a real pirate and ask him where he had buried his treasure. Surely some pirate must have visited upstate New York to find a good spot to bury his gold doubloons. Now to decide just which pirate to ask? Well, they figured there's really only one to ask: the most famous, most nefarious pirate there ever was, Captain Kidd. He had loads of treasure, and according to the stories, he buried it up and down the East Coast! Why, there were stories of treasure hunters still looking for his treasure chests that have never been found.

Deciding that that they needed a dark place to use the Ouija board, the children took their prize and went into Ann's bedroom closet. It was large enough for all four of them to fit, once they moved some shoes and a box of stuff to make room. Closing the door, it was nice and dark. They sat down in a circle, struck a match and lit the candle; its flame lit the closet in an eerie orange glow, while the burnt match lent a sulfurous smell to the darkness.

In the flickering light, they placed the board in the middle of the circle and invoked the board to speak with the ghost of Captain Kidd, the pirate. Next, they placed their fingertips on the planchette. As soon they did, it felt a bit colder in the closet, and a shiver went up Ann's spine.

Under their fingers, the planchette strained to move and spell out something. Frightened and shaking, they let go of the planchette. At that moment, the closet became ice cold. Ann was sitting with her back against the wall and began to get up. Behind Ann, from out of the wall, two large hands formed and grabbed her shoulders; big, strong, icy fingers pressed into her. She screamed as they roughly pushed her back down, holding her there. The other children began screaming, pushed the closet door open and ran downstairs. The hands let go, and Ann dashed out after the others. As she ran, Ann could have sworn she heard a deep laugh that resonated from the closet. They didn't stop until they were out of the house, still shaking and screaming.

When the children had gathered enough courage to go back upstairs to Ann's room, the Ouija board, planchette and candle were there as they had left them. They carefully returned the Ouija board to the same pile of junk by the curb. After narrowly escaping the captain's grasp, they never touched another Ouija board again. It would seem that even in death, Captain Kidd does not want to share his treasure.

WYOMING

Wyoming County, formed in 1841, was originally from part of the Holland Land Purchase in 1793. Some of the places mentioned are no longer in Wyoming County because the original division of counties were much larger, and as more people settled in western New York, they were divided into smaller counties.

Wyoming County was home of Mary Jemison, the famous "White Woman of the Genesee." Her family had settled in an area that is now central Pennsylvania, on territory that was part of the Iroquois Confederacy. The French and Indian War was raging, and raiding parties hit many of the settlements in 1758. Mary's family was murdered and scalped; only she had been spared. Eventually, the raiding party reached Fort Duquesne (present-day Pittsburgh), and Mary was sold to two Seneca Indians.

The Seneca adopted Mary, calling her Deh-he-wä-mis, which roughly meant "pretty or pleasant to look at." She married a Delaware Indian named Sheninjee. They had one child, a boy named Thomas, named after Mary's father. Not wishing to return to white society, Mary, her husband and their child headed north to the area near the Genesee Gorge. Along the way, Sheninjee became ill and died while out hunting. Mary and Thomas went on to the Seneca settlement of Little Beards Town, present-day Cuylerville, New York. There she stayed with Sheninjee's clan relatives.

She again married, this time to a Seneca named Hiakatoo; together they had six more children.

Mary was well known for her kindness and generosity. She even helped "Indian" Allan hide from the British after his scheme to help bring peace between the Seneca and the Americans. Mary also counseled the Seneca when they negotiated the Treaty of the Big Tree in Geneseo in 1797 in New York. Mary Jemison stayed with her Indian family until she died in 1833.

The Face in the Wall

Built in 1851 in an area with abundant mineral springs, the Hillside Inn was originally intended as a health spa. It had a swimming pool filled with the mineral water for the guests. In 1858, it was purchased and converted to a private residence. For the next seventy years, it remained in the same family. The family welcomed some of our nation's great artists, poets and scientists of the time. Through the years, visitors include John Muir, Susan B. Anthony and the Roosevelts.

It was reopened in 2005 as the Hillside Inn. The current owners lovingly restored the forty-room house and grounds as a bed-and-breakfast, restaurant and banquet facility.

Throughout the years, the ghost of an older lady has occasionally been seen at the mansion. It seems to be the ghost of the former owner, Lydia Avery.

I was made aware of the ghost sightings when I was asked to authenticate a photograph taken at the inn over the summer of 2008 at a wedding reception. The bride and groom were standing in front of a wall, and a ghostly face was stretching out from the wall next to them. It was as if the wall was a sheet of rubber, and someone was pressing their face into the wall from the other side. The image was indeed on the negative, and there did not appear to be any tampering.

PART IV

GENESEE COUNTRY SOUTH

HENRIETTA

Established in 1818, Henrietta was an agricultural town whose farms grew grains and vegetables.

West Henrietta Road was once known as the South Road. Even today, if you follow it, you would eventually end up in the Deep South. The original town of Henrietta was built on the South Road in 1818. As a major north–south travel route, it was a busy, well-traveled road. To service the travelers, there were many inns along the South Road. Most have been turned into private homes; others continued their tradition of hospitality, like the Cartwright Inn (sadly now closed), into modern times.

Still visible are the stone carriage steps in front of the oldest homes, steps that made it easier to climb down from a horse-drawn carriage. One house even has a fiddler's bench built into the upstairs room. Back in the day, when the house was an inn, they had a fiddler play for the entertainment of the guests.

Another house down the road from the inn was part of the Underground Railroad network; it has a secret room in the basement that was only accessible from the outside. About five miles north on West Henrietta Road was Richardson Farm, owned at the time by Dave Richardson. Richardson reportedly used his farm as an Underground Railroad station.

The Boy with a Straw Hat

Late one dark and foggy night, Gail was driving home from a friend's house down West Henrietta Road. She passed the Baptist church on Erie Station

Road. The fog was pretty thick, and she was driving a bit slowly. In the distance on the right was a young boy. He was walking along, wearing an old-fashioned cotton shirt, jeans and a straw hat.

She thought it was very strange for a boy to be walking so late and slowed her car even more to look at him. He was barefoot, as well; he looked like something out of an old painting, she thought. The boy stopped and looked at her as she slowly passed by. She could see him looking a bit quizzically at her as she went by. Glancing to the left, she saw the old carriage stop, where they used to make carriages and wagons in the 1830s. The building later became a foundry and a steam sawmill. In more modern times, it was home to several restaurants and today is a Moose Lodge. When she looked back to the boy, he was gone; the fog had swallowed up all traces of him.

Of course, there were (and still are) numerous farms along this route, and since it was a direct road north from the Deep South, it was a major route for the Underground Railroad. Seeing a ghost walking along the old South Road might not be that unusual.

The old Carriage Stop, where carriages and wagons were built. A fire destroyed the upper section and roof years ago. Where the two windows on the second floor are now were two large swinging doors so the wagons and other carriages could be rolled out and down a ramp from the second floor.

Travel the South Road on a foggy night and you may catch a glimpse of the ghost boy as he walks along. Is he wondering what had become of the horses and carriages that used to travel the road? He will disappear into the fog as he nears the carriage stop, a place he liked to visit, to watch as they made carriages and wagons, the cars and trucks of his day.

RUSH

The first settlers came into the area in 1801; in 1804, sixteen Baptist families from Connecticut decided to settle in the area. One of the first and most useful industrial additions to any newly settled and forested area is a sawmill. In 1805, Pennsylvania native Christle Thomas built the first sawmill in the area. The old sawmill was in use until 1890. By 1835, there were eight sawmills in the area.

The town of Rush was established in 1818. The local farms grew oats, wheat, corn, beans, potatoes and cabbages, as well as fruit. Local mills worked with grain, apple and sugar cane. Yes, there were also many farmers who also raised sugar cane. The cane syrup was used as a sweetener in place of molasses.

By the 1830s, there was regular stagecoach service from Geneseo, Honeoye Falls, Rush and Henrietta to Rochester. The early roads at that time were nothing more than dirt paths worn by the passage of people and wagons. In 1846, the use of plank roads was coming into fashion. Usually made from eight-foot hemlock planks, they were used to surface the ground. In those days, it would cost about $600 to plank a mile of road. The plank roads usually charged a toll because of the high cost of maintaining a wooden road. By 1870, better methods and materials were found to create and maintain roads, and the plank roads were on their way out.

Stockyards for shipping livestock were built when the railroad came through in the 1890s. It was a boon to farmers, who could more easily ship their produce and travelers. Today, Rush maintains a balance between suburban housing tracts and its rural agricultural roots.

The Gray Lady of Fishell Road

On Fishell Road, near Route 15, is a small, forgotten graveyard, with about fifteen graves. It sits on the south shore of Honeoye Creek. Only three of the headstones remain, and they are knocked down and nearly hidden in the grass.

In the summer of 2006, Sandy moved into the house across the road from the small graveyard. She liked to walk her dog, an energetic cocker spaniel named Sunny, every day along the road. One day, Sunny managed to get free and ran off. He headed right for the graves and was circling the headstones when Sandy caught up with him. As she put the leash on him, she noticed the name on one of the gravestones—"Catherine." Thinking no more about it, Sandy walked the dog home.

That evening as she lay in bed, Sandy glanced at the mirror door on the closet. Her heart skipped a beat as she watched a gray shadow silently pacing back and forth. A slight heaviness could be felt in the air as the shadow paced. The shadow was of a slender woman in a full dress. Then

Catherine's grave on Fishell Road.

the gray shadow walked past the closet and vanished. Just as the shadow vanished, the name Catherine flashed into Sandy's mind. She wondered if something had followed her home from the old graveyard the dog had run to that afternoon. The gray shadow came back to visit Sandy's room several times in the next two weeks.

Then, in the late evenings, the living room stereo began to turn on. No one was downstairs, and the dog was in her room, sleeping. Most recently, Sandy's office paper shredder turned itself on in the night; she had to unplug it to get it to turn off.

While not a regular visitor, Catherine stops by from time to time, sometimes playing with the stereo and occasionally visiting the bedroom. One recent evening, Sandy was sitting in the living room when several CD cases popped out of the CD rack onto the floor. Perhaps Catherine has a curiosity about today's music?

A recent note on Catherine's activity: in April 2009, I was visiting Sandy, and she said that there were several people looking around the cemetery that day. They seemed to be looking at the gravestones.

An interesting orb over the graves, photographed via infrared.

This photo was taken a moment later and shows what appears to be an orb near the same spot.

I asked out loud, "I wonder if they had disturbed Catherine?"

Within minutes, the XM receiver popped on. We turned to look at the receiver; there was nothing near it, and the timer had not been set. It would seem that Catherine is still dropping in for a visit now and then.

ROUTES 5 AND 20

Routes 5 and 20 originally formed an Indian footpath going east and west along the top of the Finger Lakes between Albany and Buffalo. In the 1700s, it became a wagon trail for pioneers and settlers coming from the east, and in the early 1800s, the dirt trail was improved into a more substantial road for travel. New and improved methods to grade and create a lasting road base were coming into use.

Routes 5 and 20 go from Albany to Buffalo, New York.

In more recent times, Routes 5 and 20 were a part of the transcontinental federal highway that connected Boston, Massachusetts, to Newport, Oregon, before the superhighways like the New York State Thruway were built. The route runs just north of the Finger Lakes. It meanders east across New York State though many small towns and villages—a slower and very scenic way to travel.

Phantom Tanker

Years ago, late on a cold, snowy night, a man driving a milk tanker was trying to make up for lost time due to the severe snow on Routes 5 and 20. He was hauling five thousand gallons of milk, going faster than was prudent for the weather. As he passed the occasional car or truck, in their rearview mirror they would see his headlights grow in the blinding snow and then a flash of his purple cab and silver tank as he roared passed them into the tempest.

Ghostly headlights on
a cold and snowy night
on Routes 5 and 20.

Making up time on a stormy night with icy roads tempted fate, and fate was not in a good mood that night. On one of the curves between Geneva and Bloomfield, his rig began to slide sideways as he hit the curve. Smashing through the guardrail, the truck rolled on its side. By the time help arrived, it was too late for the driver.

In 2006, Jim began to drive a newspaper delivery truck along 5 and 20. He remembers one very cold and snowy February night well. Jim was a few miles past Geneva when he saw a pair of headlights in his rearview mirror. They were coming up fast. An odd chill went through him. The headlights swung out in the passing lane. Jim glimpsed an older purple cab hauling a stainless tank. He caught a glimpse of a milk tanker as it zoomed past him, and just as it pulled ahead, it disappeared. He could see only the driving snowflakes lit up by his headlights.

If you travel Routes 5 and 20 between Geneva and Bloomfield late on a dark and cold winter night, you may see the phantom milk truck, its headlights in the mirror roaring up from behind and passing you in the left lane. You might even feel a cold chill as the phantom passes and vanishes into the icy swirls, racing to make a delivery long past due.

ABOUT THE AUTHOR

Ralph Esposito, a native of Brooklyn, New York, now calls Rochester, New York, home. He is a professional photographer, videographer, radio personality, paranormal investigator and author. His interest in the paranormal grew until 2003, when he began ghost hunting.

Esposito started doing ghost tours in Rochester, New York, as well as participating in a local cable access paranormal investigation show called *Mystic Encounters*, now in its third season and seen online at www.reparanormal.com. Ralph has spoken at several paranormal conventions and also teaches ghost hunting. He has several new paranormal book projects in the works.

Other books in the Haunted America series
from The History Press include:

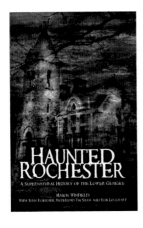  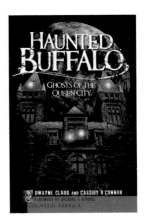

Haunted Rochester: A Supernatural History of the Lower Genesee
Mason Winfield, with John Koerner, Reverend Tim Shaw and Rob Lockhart
978.1.59629.418.9 • 6 x 9 • 128pp • $19.99

Hauntings of the Hudson River Valley: An Investigative Journey
Vincent T. Dacquino
978.1.59629.242.0 • 6 x 9 • 128pp • $19.99

Haunted Buffalo: Ghosts of the Queen City
Dwayne Claud and Cassidy O'Connor
978.1.59629.775.3 • 6 x 9 • 128pp • $19.99

To purchase, please visit www.historypress.net

 HAUNTED AMERICA